NEW LIGHT CHRISTIANS

Initiators of the Nineteenth Century Reformation

Colby D. Hall

Edited by
Bradley S. Cobb

Charleston, AR:
Cobb Publishing
2020

Published in the United States of America by:
Cobb Publishing
704 East Main St
Charleston, AR 72933
www.CobbPublishing.com
CobbPublishing@gmail.com
479-747-8372

ISBN: 978-1-947622-46-3

TABLE OF CONTENTS

PUBLISHER'S PREFACE

Most students of the Restoration know quite a bit about Alexander Campbell. Barton W. Stone is usually known for preaching in an 1801 revival at Cane Ridge (most don't know about the Pentecostal-ish goings on there), and later for joining forces with Alexander Campbell. These are probably the only two things most people know about him (if they even know those).

This book seeks to correct that—and not necessarily just putting Barton W. Stone back into his place in Restoration Movement history, but also his whole movement, which included more men than just him.

The "New Light" Christians *never* referred to themselves by that name, but the author of this book uses it as a convenient way to distinguish them from other localized groups who also called themselves "Christians" or the "Christian Church" (specifically, James O'Kelly's "Christian Church" in the south, and Abner Jones and Elias Smith's "Christian Church" or "Christian Connexion" in New England). So don't let his use of the name cloud your view of the information.

The author was connected with the Disciples of Christ, the most liberal branch of the Restoration Movement, but this fact does not come across in the following pages.

All footnotes are original to this work, except for ones marked "*Editor,*" which have been added for this updated edition.

We hope you find this work interesting and beneficial to your understanding of Restoration Movement history.

"From this period (c. 1804) I date the commencement of that reformation which has progressed to this day."
—*Barton W. Stone*

FOREWORD

It was in the early 1950's, while doing research for my work on the life story the long-neglected pioneer preacher, Rice Haggard, that I made a surprising discovery. That discovery gave me a new slant on the beginnings of the "Reformation of the Nineteenth Century."[1] It was not so much new facts, as it was a fresh approach. It was enough to convince me that students of that portion of history deserve the publication of another book.

This book is the result of this "new slant" on the history of the "Disciples of Christ."

The surprise was the large amount of reformation that occurred prior to Alexander Campbell, and from strictly American influences. Of course, I had long known and taught that the Movement got off to a very slow start in (western) Virginia; that after more than a decade they could count as theirs, less than ten congregations; and that for thirteen years they were known as Baptists.

The initial surprise came to me when I deduced that Rice Haggard, that early reforming evangelist who came out from the Methodists, had never met Alexander Campbell face to face. But more than this, in all his life (1779-1819) he had never even heard of the Campbells. Yet, Haggard's career was at the very base of the movement for Christian union. He had participated in three phases of reform. He had been with Stone in person at the very time of the first outbreaking of his reformation in 1804, which, quite obviously, was prior to the coming of the Campbells to America. He was a close co-worker with Stone; he had published the first hymn-book for the reformation, and also another book, the very first one pleading for the union of "all Christians in one church"; and for the one name "Christian." Moreover, Stone had a larger following in the

---

[1] This was a name frequently in use to describe what is better known as "The Restoration Movement" or in some 'academic' circles, "The Stone-Campbell Movement."—*Editor.*

i

South than the Campbells in the North, and when Campbell en-
larged his following by coming into Kentucky, their groups were
about equal in numbers at the time of the uniting.

It was through this experience that I was led to realize that the
first beginnings of the Movement occurred in the West of young
America; and had grown out of the vigorous stream of American
evangelism which had started in New England and had developed
in strength through the South and West in strictly American conditions; that it was out of this stream under the leadership of Barton
W. Stone, that the first break was made with the conversion pattern
of Calvinism, that this break was the most complete of any, and
was final.[2]

The story herein is the same dear story, but it will be told from
a different viewpoint and with different emphases.

Truth is like that. Oftentimes it becomes hidden in a mass of
facts, and becomes obscured. Some insights into truth are maiden-
like and must be courted.

After I retired from teaching, I found it interesting to read again
the various texts and reference books that I had used in my classes.
I knew quite well that many passages in these volumes had been
neglected; a teacher's schedule is a merciless taskmaster, especially when that teacher is also an administrator.

In W.A. Fortune's *Disciples in Kentucky*, I encountered again,
"The historians have not given the contribution of this section
(Kentucky) the notice it merits." That struck a responsive chord in
my mind, as it applied to the story of the "conversion experience"
of Barton Stone. This was the experience which started him on the
line of thinking that gave slow birth to the reformation. He tells it
feelingly in his *Autobiography*. But this rare volume was available

---

[2] The author would have done well to do more research, and seen the impact
and influence of the New England Christians (often called the Christian Connex-
ion/Connection), particularly Abner Jones, who came to the same conclusions as
did Stone, and established congregations based on a thoroughly *un*denomina-
tional approach as early as 1801.—*Editor.*

to few people and has not been utilized by the authors in the field as it deserves. My observation indicates that W.G. West relates more of Stone's conversion "agony" than any other; but he does not elucidate the point which challenged me. This story may be found in Chapter III herein, and its follow-up in Chapter IV.

In several other paragraphs I have let slip out something of the highest esteem in which I hold the authors in this field, and their works. I have the impulse to add much more. Concerning the authors of the history texts which I have been teaching these years, I desire to express appreciation. Most of them have been my cherished companions through the passing years.

Among the authors in the field of Disciples' history who have aided and inspired me, I may mention some: first, the one who is universally recognized as the number one, Dr. W.E. Garrison, a genuine philosopher; (I treasure the memory of my personal acquaintance with his revered father, J.H. Garrison); then his student and co-author, A.T. DeGroot, bright and stimulating (one-time secretary to my former co-laborer, Frederick D. Kershner), and my present successor as Professor of Church History in Brite College of the Bible; C.C. Ware, stimulating and challenging, with whom I have much more correspondence than face-to-face meetings (I have welcomed many of his North Carolina preacher-boys to Brite).

Then, there is Wm. G. West, one of three brilliant sons of a beloved pioneer, ground-breaking evangelist, an associate in the Disciples of Christ Historical Society, and a Barton W. Stone author; and his brother W. Fred West, one-time my fellow faculty member in Brite, who has added a valuable work to the Disciples books.

Then, I cherish the fact that several of my former pupils have become authors and executives in whom I take delight. There is Perry Gresham, whose brilliant intellect and charming personality I recognized in its youthful evolvement and sought to encourage, and I now rejoice in his present position as the President of the old college of Alexander Campbell's founding; D. Ray Lindley, for a while President of Atlantic Christian College, now President of T.C.U., whom I chose as my successor in 1947, as Dean of Brite College; James Moudy, now Dean of the Graduate School of T.C.U., was an outstanding student in my class and whom I followed with interest and pride through his graduate work in Duke; Noel Keith, who succeeded me as Professor of Church History, also of Bible; until he was called to be the Head of Undergraduate Bible in T.C.U.; also, he has been most helpful to me as the Director of the T.C.U. Press; and as a climax, Granville Walker, my former student, fellow professor, a fellow elder, a top flight pulpiteer, my family's beloved pastor for fifteen years, our favorite preacher, and a genuine adviser.

When I think of the patience and encouragement used by my wife, Beatrice Tomlinson Hall (T.C.U. B.A. '08) and my daughter, Dr. Bita May Hall (T.C.U. '31, M.A. '33, Ph.D. Columbia '51) I must express my hearty thanks, and recognition of their really valuable help.

I am grateful to the multitude of students who have been in my classes, these years, and grateful also, for their records of service, so many in high positions; to each and all I hereby extend my appreciation and gratitude—with the remark that if it were not for detracting from the value of the text books I would say that "Probably I learned more from you than I taught you." Garrulous, am I? Remember, I am now an octogenarian. Be careful, boys, don't pronounce that word "octogeranium." (Still an octogenarian, you see).

Colby D. Hall

CHAPTER I
HISTORICAL PERSPECTIVE

THIS VOLUME is not designed to be a history of the entire Movement. Its scope is only the period during which the "New Light Christians," a group which was active under the leadership of Barton W. Stone, existed and grew for more than two decades before merging with the Campbells.

Neither is it to be another biography of Barton W. Stone; the two biographies of him (Ware's and West's) are excellently done, supplement each other, and, in general, cover the ground. Familiarity with these will greatly help the reader to follow this book with understanding. It will add emphasis at certain points.

This book is an attempt to record the history, features, contribution, and spirit of that early period of the Reformation of the Nineteenth Century, from 1800 through 1832, with the emphasis on the American phases of reform. It shows that the Movement originated in America, on an American background, and was shaped, in its early phases, by American thinkers.

As intimated in the "Foreword" above, the standard pattern of the history of this Movement, heretofore, has portrayed it as originating and centering in the East, about the Campbells, its background largely Scottish and British, its problems for the most part imported, as were its leaders, three of the "big four."[1] This picture is not necessarily wrong, but it is surely incomplete.

Its chief flaw is that the actual initiatory steps of the Movement which occurred in Kentucky in 1804 are treated as though they occurred later and were minor and ancillary. We will show that these were earlier, initiatory, rising out of conditions that were native to America, striking at the heart of American conditions that needed correction. These will appear as the story proceeds.

---

[1] These "Big Four" are: Thomas Campbell, Alexander Campbell, Barton W. Stone, and Walter Scott.—*Editor.*

The pronouncement by the Secessionist Scottish Presbyterian, Thomas Campbell, in 1809, that the "church of Christ on earth is essentially, intentionally and constitutionally one," was ecumenical, timely, and, historically, was one of the early utterances on the theme. But it was not the earliest. Five years prior to the issuance of the "Declaration and Address," there had been issued, on the western frontier of America, a document just as ecumenical, and just as apt, by a native American[2] who got his inspiration from the completely American scene.

Thomas Campbell and Barton W. Stone were men of similar characteristics and kindred souls, as suggested by the spirit of their two documents: gentle, sweet-spirited, pacific, and ecumenically minded. But the son, Alexander, turned the current of that Movement in a different direction. His aim was not ecumenical (at least only incidentally so). It was "restoration of the ancient order."

The fusion of the two in 1832 was, we believe, inevitable, Providential, and due to Stone more than to either of the Campbells.

As stated above the record of Stone's life, as a pioneer and preacher has been published, excellently (though belatedly), by C.C. Ware;[3] Stone's leadership as "Early Advocate of Christian Unity" has been well developed by Wm. G. West.[4] Now the story of the entire "New Light Movement" as the initial step in the current reform is called for. This present book undertakes to respond to that call.

This is done in full recognition of the previous works and the contributions of the actors in the earlier stories. The historical accounts of the Movement as a whole, especially the completest one,

---

[2] By this, the author does not mean an "Indian," (as is the modern usage of this term) but just someone who was born in America.—*Editor.*

[3] Ware, Charles Crossfield. *Barton Warren Stone, a Biography.* St. Louis: The Bethany Press, 1932.

[4] West, William Garrett. *Barton Warren Stone: Early American Advocate of Christian Unity.* Nashville: The Disciples of Christ Historical Society, 1954.

Garrison and DeGroot,[5] have given as much attention to the "New Lights," as would naturally be expected. But a new light is now available on the "New Lights." Let's bring it to light.

The aim of this volume is not displacement, but merely completion, not correcting so much as filling in the gaps; also, it is desired to recognize more of the features, problems, and spirit of bold, brash, young America on its migration to the West, intoxicated, maybe, with its interpretation of the spirit of freedom, but balanced by its recognition of the authority of the Scriptures. This was in the period when it was on its way to the West, migrating, unsettled, venturesome, striving vigorously and sincerely to shake itself free from the vice-like grip of the theology of Calvinism. That break away from the contradictions of Calvinism was much earlier and more complete than the Campbells' and perhaps was the most distinct and meritorious contribution of Stone and the "New Light Christian" group.

This group has not so far, been clearly delineated as a distinct group, with a specific contribution of its own. Each author, as a rule, has been primarily concerned with the final combined group and its ultimate achievements, so that these earlier movers have been subdued. Let us, herein, treat these American early beginners as arising *ab initio*, out of their own American frontier, beginning a movement out of their own American background, solving their own problems on the frontier before they knew of any other company of reformers. This very thing was done by Barton Stone, Rice Haggard, David Purviance, and their fellow laborers and had a multitude of plain "Christians" pleading for the union of all churches in one body years before they were aware of the other company pleading for a return to the New Testament pattern.

In presenting this early group of "New Light Christians," it seems well to include the (condensed) biographies of several typi-

---

[5] Garrison, W.E., and DeGroot, Alfred T. *The Disciples of Christ, a History.* St. Louis: Christian Board of Publication, 1948. Revised edition, 1958.

cal leaders among them, who have not been, heretofore, much pub-
licized, or whose published biographies are now not readily acces-
sible.[6]

The plain historical fact is that the fusion of the two groups into
one, in 1832 and thereafter, was so complete that the earlier group
of "Christians" became unduly obscured. Indeed, so thorough was
the fusion of the two that it became easy and customary for students of this Movement to assume that all of the features of the
combined Movement had been in both camps from the beginning.
This is distinctly not the case.

For practical purposes, it would be well to be grateful for the
perfect fusion, and continue to neglect the earlier group. But this
conclusion will not satisfy the historian. That earlier period is a
part of Early American Church History and should be clarified and
recorded. That is the earnest desire of the present volume.

It became necessary to find a name by which to refer to this
distinctive historical group. The appellation used by their contem-
poraries was "New Lights." These good people rejected this name,
as they did all names other than the one: "Christian."

With all due deference to their position and accepting it heartily, we use the term here (always in quotation marks) because it is
distinctive and clear—and, in this case, practical and time-saving.
But in doing so let us review the origins and usages of the phrase,
"New Lights," so we may understand how it came to be applied to
them.

The term has become so general in use that it has found its way
into the dictionaries, signifying, "one who accepts new (usually
liberal) doctrine or views."[7] It came to America from Scotland
where the Secessionist Presbyterians divided into "New Lights"
and "Auld Lights" for obvious reasons. Naturally these also subdi-

---

[6] Many of these biographies have recently been brought back into print by
the publisher of this volume.—*Editor.*

[7] "New Light," Webster's New International Dictionary of the English Language (2nd ed., unabridged, Springfield, Mass.: G. & C. Merriam Co., 1943).

vided. Thomas Campbell was an Anti-burgher, Auld Licht, Seces-sionist Presbyterian.

The term was picked up again during the First Great Awaken-ing in America to designate a group of Presbyterian preachers in Pennsylvania, who were more zealous for evangelism and less rig-id in the educational requirements for their preachers than the old brethren. Those forward-looking ministers and scholars who influ-enced Stone's early years, Patillo, Caldwell, Hodge, Craighead et al., were of this school of "New Light" Presbyterian versus the "Old Side" under the hard and fast orthodox leader, Dr. David Rice. It was quite easy, therefore, for the populace to fix on the Stone group this appellation, "New Lights," for they had some "new ideas." Their opponents used several much more harsh and objectionable epithets.

A clarifying example of the ready use of the term in an earlier period is to be found in its use by Professor John Vant Stephens of the Lane Seminary (Cincinnati, 1910-1932). He published in 1942, a small volume (28 pages), on the topic, "The New Lights (The Christian Church)." His purpose was to make a clear distinction between that body and the Cumberland Presbyterian Church. They both developed about the same time and in the same region, and some folks, he thought, had confused them as being identical.

As a matter of interest (and of record) let us present here the words of Barton W. Stone on the usage of names.

> We have taken the name "Christian," not because we considered ourselves more pure than others—but because we knew it was the name first given to the disciples of Je-sus by Divine authority. It better agreed with our spirit, which is to unite with all Christians, without regard to names or distinctions. There are party names too many al-ready in the world, without our assuming another. But our brethren, unwilling for us to bear that name, have given us others we will not own—as "New Lights" and "Schismat-ics." The name "New Lights" is not novel. It was long ago given to Whitefield, to Wesley, to the former Methodists, to

the first Baptists in Virginia, and indeed to every sect of living Christians in my remembrance for years past. To be called by the name of such worthies we need not blush. But this name, the least of all others, agrees with our profession. We have professed no new light—but the old unsullied light which shines in the Bible.[8]

The end of the "New Light" period came with the union of the two groups of Stone and Campbell into the united Movement. In our endeavor herein, to draw a picture of the earlier group, we shall re-tell the life stories of a number of personalities, men whose published biographies may be rare. To this purpose Ch. XIII, herein, is devoted. Several of these died before the fusion of the groups, hence were "New Light" features. Others tell plainly of the changes in their views as they progressed into the Union. These experiences clearly show up the differences. At least two of three persons, although exposed to the views of the Campbell group, rejected them and persisted in remaining in the "New Light" Persuasion.[9]

We will not present a theoretical analysis of their teachings and practices, but will rather let their features show up out of the experiences of the actors themselves.

Of course, the attitudes of the recognized leader of the group, Barton W. Stone, will need to be discussed and compared with those of the leader of the other group, Alexander Campbell. The ultimate eminence of the latter is recognized and analyzed in Chapter XII.

This word should be added: the unusually lengthy quotations from Stone's autobiography are done deliberately, by reason of the scarcity of that old book. At the time of this writing [1959], it is to be found only in the libraries of colleges and Seminary institutions.

---

[8] From the "Address to Christians," circulated by Stone in 1814 and published in *Works of Elder B. W. Stone*, edited and published by Elder James M. Mathes (Cincinnati: Wiltstach & Keys Co., 1859), p. 159.
[9] See later chapters of this work for more information.

Yet it records so brilliantly the wonderful spirit of the man as well as the details of his career. It should be re-printed if that were financially feasible.[10]

---

[10] *The Autobiography of Barton W. Stone* has been republished, and is available from the publisher of this work, via their website or Amazon.com.—*Editor.*

CHAPTER II
THE REFORMATION OF THE NINETEENTH CENTURY GREW OUT OF THE REVIVALS OF THE EIGHTEENTH

THE REFORMATION of the Nineteenth Century represents the further development of the principles of the Protestant Reformation of the Sixteenth. This may be said, and has been said, of other genuine reform movements. But as we trace out the history of the development of these principles, it is worthwhile to observe that the errors left over in Protestantism have had much to do with the shaping these doctrines.

This chapter is devoted to the tracing out of two of these prominent errors left over in Protestantism from the Sixteenth Century Reformation, and observing some decisive effects they had on the development of the Reformation Movement of the Nineteenth Century.

One of these "errors" of Protestantism, brought over from the medieval Church, is that of the Established Church concept. We Protestants owe much to Luther, and we gladly acknowledge it. But we owe to him also the "error" of retaining the State Church concept. It is quite likely that his loyalty to the German princess of State kept him from being a martyr, so we cannot quarrel with him. The concept came, or remained, also in England. And from there was transplanted to colonial America.[1]

It was in connection with its general tendency to lower moral standards of conduct among the general populace that the effect of the State Church concept was severely felt. We rightly praise the first comers to the new continent for their lofty ideals of seeking God rather than just gold, but history makes it plain that the suc-

---

[1] In Connecticut the Congregationalist was the State Church until 1818, in New Hampshire until 1817, and in Massachusetts until 1833.

ceeding generations were deeply absorbed in more earthly pursuits. Perhaps we may say, in their defense, that such mundane pursuits were essential: finding better land, staking out homes for the family, defending against savages and savage conditions, assuring the temporal future of the posterity, and such. In any event, the fact that moral standards did drift to a lower level was observable by all, and especially by the sincere preachers.

Now the influence of the State Church concept on this condition was not helpful. Sad to say, it was the opposite; it was definitely deleterious. That was for lack of motivation. Every child was born a citizen of the state, and also a member of the State Church. That was without its consent, or any commitment. Hence, the relationship with the church came to be mostly routine and formal. To multitudes it meant nothing vital, except that it was necessary for voting and paying taxes. The historians concur in saying that not more than ten percent of the population even acknowledged any interest in the church.

Many of the clergy were content with the formal observance of the services, it is true, but many more of them were truly and sincerely distressed on account of the low moral tone of the people.

One of the latter kinds was Jonathan Edwards (1703-58), one of the most brilliant scholars of the day, and the one who gained recognition as the most outstanding philosopher of early America. He is usually credited with having initiated the revival of religion in 1734, known as the Great Awakening, although it was started eight years earlier. Edwards recorded his picture of the degradation of morals in his own city of Northhampton, Massachusetts:

> Licentiousness greatly prevailed among the youth of the town; there were many of them addicted to night walking and frequenting the tavern, and lewd practices whereby some, by their example, exceedingly corrupted others. It was their manner to get together in assemblies of both sexes, for mirth and jollity, which they called frolics; and they would often spend the greater part of the night in them,

without regard to order in the families they belonged to: indeed family government did too much fail in the town.[2]

This low state of morals, and general indifference to religion greatly distressed the hearts of the sincere preachers, generally, and stirred them to try to discover the best means and message to win the allegiance of the people to God and religion.

The reader will please observe that this urgency of evangelism to combat the moral lapse continued to be the motivation through many a generation of the great revivals. But there was a complication which greatly hampered the success of the revivals. That was the other "error" brought over into Protestantism, and it was a powerful influence. That was the doctrines of Calvinism. John Calvin, recognized as the most profound thinker of the Sixteenth Century, and a good man beyond question, nevertheless left a system of theology that was hard to apply in evangelism. Philip Schaff, the great church historian says of it, in his multi-volume church history:

> Calvinism has the advantage of logical compactness and completeness. Admitting its premises, it is difficult to escape its conclusions. A system can only be overthrown by a system. It requires a theological genius of the order of Augustine and Calvin, who shall rise above antagonism of divine sovereignty and human freedom and shall lead on to a system built upon the rock of the historic Christ, and inspired from beginning to end with the love of God to all mankind.[3]

Its major premise was total human depravity; its minor, human impotence. John Calvin was well aware of the extreme domination of the papal system over the Church and over European culture. He endeavored to overcome this by making the sovereignty of God the

---

[2] W.W. Sweet, *The Story of Religion in America* (Revised edition, New York: Harper & Bros., 1939), p. 187.

[3] Philip Schaff, *History of the Christian Church* (New York: Charles Scribner's Sons) Vol. VII (1898), p. 187.

basis of his theological system. In doing this he stressed it to such an unreasonable and unscriptural extreme that he left no room for the Biblical teachings on the freedom of man. The deterministic element[4] in Calvinism, based on the doctrine of original sin and total hereditary depravity, provided for election, limited atonement, and the absolute impotence of man.

It was the teaching on the impotence of man that balked the revival efforts. The preachers had to announce that the sinner could do absolutely nothing toward his salvation; he must wait until he felt the Holy Spirit come into his heart and, by a supernatural action which he could feel, give him faith. This hard doctrine was preached by the Puritans of New England in all its harshness; and it seemed for a while to go unquestioned. It tended to block the earnest evangelistic efforts of the New England preachers.

Now Scotland had become the home of Calvinism, transplanted there by that doughty fighter, John Knox. In that land of stubborn minds, Calvinism met no challenge. Even Robert Sandeman, who espoused the Lockian concept that belief was based on evidence, agreed as a good Calvinist, that "Only those who are elected to salvation by the sovereign good pleasure of God, can perform the rational act of believing the evidence about Jesus Christ."[5]

It was in America that this restrictive Calvinism was challenged. (Here the worth of the individual had been re-discovered.) And when that challenge came it arose in the West, from the voice of the earliest advocate of the "Reformation of the Nineteenth Century," in the year 1801. The challenger was a humble evangelist by the name of Barton Warren Stone.[6]

---

[4] I discriminate the "deterministic element" in order to avoid seeming to counter all of Calvinism. He had many permanent elements, for good.

[5] W.E. Garrison and A.T. DeGroot, *The Disciples of Christ: A History* (St. Louis: Christian Board of Publication, 1948), p. 49.

[6] Abner Jones, of whom the author seems unaware, made the same break with Calvinism no later than 1801, and likely a year or two earlier, in Vermont.—*Editor.*

That challenge appeared only after a long, long struggle. It was a long way from Jonathan Edwards in 1734 to Barton W. Stone in 1801.

And it will require of us a somewhat detailed journey to be able to appreciate the background of his challenge. But this journey the reader must make with us, in order to understand why this humble preacher on the western frontier could, must, and did challenge the teachings of such great scholars as John Calvin and Jonathan Edwards. So let us now take a rapid review of the Revivals of the Eighteenth Century, considered, as usual, in three periods: the Great Awakening (following 1726 or 1734); the Second Awakening (following 1790); and the Great Western Revival (1800 and after).[7]

Throughout this story, it should be borne in mind that the dominating motivation of these revivalists was the consecrated desire to save the souls of the people, eternally, and to elevate the common level of moral living among the people. Meanwhile, the anti-revival preachers were regularly droning along with the dry, orthodox theological doctrines by the hours.

The standard theology pictured the sufferings of the unregenerated as of the severest sort. They were condemned to burn in the fiery pits of hell forever. Edwards' sermon on "Sinners in the hands of an angry God" is said to have made his listeners cling to the pews to keep from slipping off into the fiery pit which he pictured to them. The usual preacher, conscious of the sinfulness of the people was inclined to pour on the threats, heavily. Such "hell fire and damnation" preaching was calculated to scare the sinner out of hell.

---

[7] This is not intended as a history of Evangelism; it is only a review. If the reader desires to review the history, these books are recommended: Joseph Tracy, *A History of the Revival of Religion in the Times of Jonathan Edwards and George Whitefield*, (Boston: Tappan & Dennet, 1842); W.W. Sweet, *Op. cit.* and his *Revivalism in America* (New York: Charles Scribner's Sons, 1944).

And yet, what could the poor sinner do? He was told that there was nothing he could do, that the first move must be made by the Holy Spirit, coming into his heart by supernatural power to give him faith. This contradiction balked the sinner and discouraged the preacher.

But these preachers were not easily discouraged. They figured out some theory. First, Edwards is said to have evolved a theory: that "a man had the power to act in accordance with the choice of his mind, but with the origin of the inclination he had nothing to do."[8]

Whatever the philosopher intended that to mean, we may be sure that the seeking sinner was not helped by it. Another scheme was figured out, known as the "means" theory. It was taught and zealously practiced, that although the seeker could do nothing, nevertheless some "means" could be used to help him. These "means" turned out to be such practices as praying, coaxing, counseling, exhorting, pleading with, singing. All of this would surely stir up the emotions, at least. And it did!

This "means" theory was developed by the second generation, including Jonathan Edwards Jr., Samuel Hopkins, and others. They were known as Neo-Edwardians or Hopkinsonians. The strict Calvinists were not only cold to the revivals, they opposed them vigorously. Perhaps much of their objections was to the "enthusiasm" engendered, and some to the noisy exhibitionism which often accompanied the emotionalism.

Historians in general have dated the beginning of the Revival as 1734, with Edwards in Northampton, Massachusetts. But eight years prior to that time a revival had broken out in the Raritan valley in New Jersey, under the preaching of Theodore Freylinghuysen, a Dutch Reformed Pietist. And it was in the West that the revivals had their greatest sway.

At about the same time a center of Presbyterian evangelistic in-

---

[8] Sweet, *Religion in America*, p. 197.

fluence began in the labors of Rev. William Tennent, pastor at Neshaminy, Pennsylvania. Here, he established a school which he used to educate his four sons for the ministry, and also gathered in other ministerial students. This was the beginning of the famous "Log College" type of training, saving the cost and concern of sending the boys to the Eastern Universities.

The Scotch-Irish Presbyterians were strong in Pennsylvania, and their settlements stretched southward, through western Virginia into North Carolina and later Tennessee and Kentucky. The heart of their message was evangelism; hence they took up the "means" party attitude. Their evangelism was warm and active. The "Old Side," strict Calvinists among these Scotch Presbyterians were cold to the revivalist. They held high education standards for their ministers. In order to counter the tendency to educate ministers in these local schools, such as the "Log Colleges," the Philadelphia Synod passed a rule requiring of candidates, a classical education and in a British or Eastern College, such as Yale or Harvard. This issue caused a definite break in the Presbyterian ranks.

Gilbert Tennent, the first "Log College" product, was located at New Brunswick where the New Brunswick Presbytery had its meetings. It was made up mostly of graduates of the "Log Colleges." The tension became so strong that the Synod of Philadelphia, in 1741, expelled the New Brunswick Presbytery for its stand on the lower qualifications of the education of the ministry. However, Gilbert Tennent's own irenic disposition had much to do with the reuniting of the two groups, by the formation of the Synod of New York and Philadelphia in 1758.

But the spirit of the New Side lived on in the revival spirit of the "Log College" preachers, of whom there was a goodly number; and they proved to be leaders of strong caliber and much influence, as we shall see. One of these, John Rowland, made a notable change in the themes of his preaching. Instead of dwelling on the wrath of God he emphasized "inviting and encouraging subjects such as the infinite love and pity of God." This proved to be a "means" of drawing many converts. The preaching of two broth-ers, Samuel and John Blair, had powerful effects on their hearers. Often some would be overcome and fainting, others deeply sob-bing, others crying in almost dolorous manner. There appeared al-so some unusual "Bodily Exercises," much after the fashion that occurred later in Kentucky and Tennessee. Samuel Blair then opened a school, similar to the Log College, and one of his gradu-ates became a powerful preacher and a skillful leader. He was Samuel Davies, the one who opened up Virginia to the Presbyteri-ans, by his diplomacy, skill and wise dealings with the state au-thorities. He later became the President of the College of New Jer-sey, the forerunner of Princeton Seminary and University.

Others of this "New Side" pattern of Presbyterian preachers in whom this story is interested are three North Carolina preachers. One is David Caldwell, a native of Lancaster, Pennsylvania, pastor of two Presbyterian churches, a graduate of Princeton (1761), the Head of the Academy in which Barton W. Stone was educated. Another was the venerable Henry Patillo, preacher at Alamance, and the one in charge of the licensing of the young preachers, whose liberalism was so helpful to them. A third was James McGready, (1790-1817) the younger man who was born in Penn-sylvania, and was educated in one of the "Log Colleges" of that state, but had lived during his youth in Guilford County, North Carolina and did his preaching there. He was to be the preacher who drove Stone into the depths of despondency, by his preaching of the threat of hell; he was also the one who set off the Western Revival, by his preaching in Logan County, Kentucky, where the excitement of the bodily exercises in extreme form first became notorious.

As the revivals moved westward, they broke out among the set-tlers, who had left their old associations and restraints back home and were foot-loose, seeking homes and financial opportunity. They were more expressive, more emotional.

It was in this region that the theories of Calvinism encountered new forms of opposition and modification. One of these was from the Methodists, for they developed in the new regions better than the old. Being Arminians in theology, they believed that Christ died for all, and they preached "free Grace," which was warmly received. But they required a personal regenerating "experience" as evidence of regenerating grace. Therefore, the same difficulty arose: the sinner could not make the first move; that must come from the supernatural visitation of the Holy Spirit.

The other break was with the Cumberland Presbyterians. This occurred in the Cumberland district of South Kentucky. This, also, was over the desire for a lower standard of education for their preachers. For the demand for preaching by the revivalists was greater than the supply. The Presbytery of the Cumberland had several quite capable preachers, who had no basic classical education, and were short on seminary courses. But they could carry on effective revivals among the poorly educated settlers. When turned down by the synod on this issue, they turned the Cumberland Presbytery into the Cumberland Presbyterian Church. They revised the creed and their practice, somewhat. They rejected election and predestination; calling it "fatalism." But they retained the requirement of the "experience" of the new birth, that is the Holy Spirit must come into the heart of the sinner and regenerate it. They declared that the sinner must have an "experience," and be able "to tell the time when and the place where it occurred." This left the "seeker" in the same predicament: unable to make a move.

As the revival movement traveled westward it met conditions conducive to its growth. The moral conditions were bad, even worse than further east. The preachers, as they moved into the new frontier, observed this fact. One typical quotation is here recorded, to give the general impression. This is the testimony of David Rice, a leading pioneer Old Side Presbyterian in Kentucky:

> After I had been here some weeks and had preached at several places, I found scarcely one man and but few women who supported a credible profession of religion. Some

were grossly ignorant of the first principles of religion. Some were given to quarreling and fighting, some to profane swearing, some to intemperance, and perhaps most of them (were) totally negligent of the forms of religion in their own homes.[9]

Thus the preachers encountered the same low grade of morality, which challenged their zeal for an intense appeal to the people to respond to the call for conversion. They met, also, conditions conducive to the high level of emotionalism, which soon marked the revivalism in the western frontier. The settlers, cut loose from their old neighborhoods, were now far-scattered and lonely. The gathering in large companies for religious services—or for any purpose—was welcome. And in these crowds, emotional expression came easy, especially to those, most of them, with a low average of education and culture. The mildness of the climate easily suggested the gathering in camps, and mass evangelism by preaching and singing was heart-warming and welcome. This style of neighborhood gathering for religious worship, with its warmth of feeling, became quite popular, and even more; it became habitual, a way of life on the frontier. It developed the features of a folk-way of the people. It gave them a lift which no cold-hearted, logical style of preaching could satisfy.

This was the kind of folk-way in which Barton W. Stone grew up. In this atmosphere he met the hard Calvinistic doctrine, had his "experience" with it, and by his struggle developed a new type of experience, more in harmony with human psychology and Scriptural instruction. Of his "experience" the next chapter will tell.

---

[9] Wm. G. West, *Barton Warren Stone: Early American Advocate of Christian Unity* (Nashville: The Disciples of Christ Historical Society, 1954).

CHAPTER III
AN "EXPERIENCE" THAT REVEALED THE INADEQUACIES OF CALVINISM AND REQUIRED A NEW PATTERN OF CONVERSION

WHEN BARTON WARREN STONE, at the age of 18, enrolled in David Caldwell's Academy in 1790, he presented an unusual example of an unprejudiced, uncommitted, open-minded person.[1] His most distinct allegiance was to America. His forefathers for five generations were American. His father, John Stone, deceased when Barton was three, had been too old to be a Revolutionary soldier; his older brothers had responded readily to the call, and served near their home in Southern Virginia.

Religiously, Barton was perhaps a perfect "neutral." He was devoid of any entangling alliances or any pressing mold of thought. That was possible because his parents, being citizens of Maryland, were automatically members of the Church of England, without any personal commitments. Barton, himself, had been "sprinkled" by a priest of the Established Church, without his awareness of it or any commitments. The other denominations he encountered casually and unconcerned; his status was, assumedly, fixed. Doubtless, he was unaware of such bodies of thought as Calvinism, Arminianism, deism and such.

Not only was he neutral in religion: he had motivation for avoiding any ties with it. His one dominating purpose in life, at this stage, was to become a qualified lawyer. That was a worthy and

---

[1] Stone, *Autobiography*, p. 7. (Note: all page numbers cited in this work are from the completely reformatted 2019 edition of Stone's *Autobiography* from this publisher.) A knowledge of the facts of his life is assumed. If the reader has not this knowledge, it might be well to read either C. C. Ware's or W. G. West's account.

approved ambition in that day and neighborhood; for behold his neighbors: Thomas Jefferson, Patrick Henry, and such. To borrow a phrase from the philosopher Locke he was *"tabula rasa,"* a clean slate, on which the years would write.

Stone possessed an energetic mind, a clean life, and devotion to truth, but without any set pattern which he was devoted to defend. He was a harp on which the winds of thought, philosophy, and religion might play, freely.

In this naive state of mind, he yielded, one evening, to the polite invitation of his room-mate, Benjamin McReynolds, to attend religious services on the campus. The visiting evangelist, James McGready, was then little known, but later, to be famous—and a friend. He had been educated in Pennsylvania, in one of those "Log Colleges" of the New Side Presbyterians, which were devoted to the "means" type of conversion. But they, as all, were still devoted to the deterministic interpretation of Calvinism and preached what was known as "hell fire and damnation" theology, like Jonathan Edwards had done. The earnest-minded Stone was greatly impressed—and depressed. Let him tell the story himself, as he wrote it down in his autobiography.[2] No other report could so well convey the idea of his utter sincerity, submission to God, and his determination to please Him.

> I consented, and walked with him. A crowd of people had assembled—the preacher came—it was James McGready, whom I had never seen before. He rose and looked around on the assembly. His person was not prepossessing, nor his appearance interesting, except his remarkable gravity, and small piercing eyes. His coarse tremulous voice excited in me the idea of something unearthly. His gestures were *sui generis*, the perfect reverse of elegance. Every thing appeared by him forgotten, but the salvation of souls. Such earnestness—such zeal—such powerful persuasion, enforced by the joys of heaven and miseries of hell, I

---

[2] Ibid., pp. 8-9.

had never witnessed before. My mind was chained by him, and followed him closely in his rounds of heaven, earth and hell, with feelings indescribable. His concluding remarks were addressed to the sinner to flee the wrath to come without delay. Never before had I comparatively felt the force of truth. Such was my excitement, that had I been standing, I should have probably sunk to the floor under the impression.

The meeting over, I returned to my room. Night coming on, I walked out into an old field, and seriously reasoned with myself on the all-important subject of religion. What shall I do? Shall I embrace religion now, or not? I impartially weighed the subject, and counted the cost. If I embrace religion, I must incur the displeasure of my dear relatives, lose the favor and company of my companions— become the object of their scorn and ridicule—relinquish all my plans and schemes for worldly honor, wealth, and preferment, and bid a final adieu to all the pleasure in which I had lived, and hoped to live on earth. Are you willing to make this sacrifice to religion? No, no, was the answer of my heart. Then the alternative is, you must be damned. Are you willing to be damned—to be banished from God—from heaven—from all good—and suffer the pains of eternal fire? No, no, responded my heart—I cannot endure the thought. After due deliberation, I resolved from that hour to seek religion at the sacrifice of every earthly good, and immediately prostrated myself before God in supplication for mercy.

According to the preaching and the experience of the pious in those days I anticipated a long and painful struggle before I should be prepared to come to Christ, or in the language then used, before I should get religion. This anticipation was completely realized by me. For one year I was tossed on the waves of uncertainty—laboring, praying, and striving to obtain saving faith—sometimes desponding, and almost despairing of ever getting it.

The doctrines then publicly taught were, that mankind were totally depraved, that they could not believe, repent, nor obey the gospel—that regeneration was an immediate work of the Spirit, whereby faith and repentance were wrought in the heart. These things were portrayed in vivid colors, with all earnestness and solemnity. Now was not then—the accepted time—now was not then, the day of salvation; but it was God's own sovereign time, and for that time the sinner must wait.[3]

And Stone did wait, for at least a year, in agony of spirit, hoping for that "experience" which God alone could send. There was nothing that he, as a human, could do, according to the Calvinistic theology. He was caught in the grip of frustration; he must move, but he was impotent; God must move first.

In this unsettled state he attended another service and heard a sermon from President J.B. Smith of Hambden-Sydney College on "The sacrifices of God are a broken spirit; a broken and a contrite heart, O God, Thou wilt not despise." He wrote: "In his description of a broken and contrite heart, I felt my own described." President Smith urged "all of this character" to approach the Lord's table that day, on pain of his sore displeasure." And this, Stone did, with some sense of satisfaction.

That evening he heard another sermon from "the honest James McGready," of much the same type as the former one by him. The text was "Tekel, Thou art weighed in the balance and found wanting." Then Stone:

> Before he closed his discourse, I had lost all hope—and feeling, and had sunk into an indescribable apathy. He soon afterward inquired of me the state of my mind. I honestly told him. He labored to arouse me from my torpor by the terrors of God, the horrors of hell. I told him his labors were lost upon me—that I was entirely callous. He left me in this gloomy state, without one encouraging word.
>
> In this state I remained for several weeks. I wandered alone—my strength failed. My relatives in Virginia heard of my situation and sent for me. My altered appearance

---

[3] Ibid., p. 9.

surprised them.[4]

After this discouraging blocking of the way to a conversion experience, he returned to the Academy in the same state of mind. Then came a somewhat different experience, which gave him a temporary hold on an edge of faith—though not yet a satisfactory "conversion."

> Soon after, I attended a meeting at Alamance, in Guilford County. Great was the excitement among the people. On the Lord's Day evening a strange young preacher, William Hodge, addressed the people. His text I shall never forget, "God is love." With much animation, and with many tears he spoke of the love of God to sinners and of what that love had done for sinners. My heart warmed with love for that lovely character described, and momentary hope and joy would rise in my troubled breast. My mind was absorbed in the doctrine—to me it appeared new. But the common admonition, "Take heed lest you be deceived," would quickly repress them. This cannot be the mighty work of the spirit, which you must experience—that instantaneous work of Almighty power, which, like an electric shock, is to renew the soul and bring it to Christ.
>
> The discourse being ended, I immediately retired to the woods alone with my Bible. Here I read and prayed with various feelings, between hope and fear. But the truth I had just heard, "God is love," prevailed. Jesus came to seek and save the lost—"Him that cometh unto me, I will in no wise cast out." I yielded and sunk at his feet a willing subject. I loved Him—I adored Him—I praised Him aloud in the silent night,—in the echoing grove around. I confessed to the Lord my sin and folly in disbelieving His work so long— and in following so long the devices of men. I now saw that a poor sinner was as much authorized to believe in Jesus at first, as at last—that now was the accepted time, and day of salvation.
>
> From this time till I finished my course of learning, I

---

[4] Ibid.

lived devoted to God.[5]

This presentation of a "God of love" was a precious relief to the nineteen or twenty-year-old Stone, when he had previously been depressed by the wrath and the threat of hell. But still he experienced no real release. It was all vague. He saw only "men as trees walking." He did see, in the direction in which he was ultimately to go, this much: "I now saw that a poor sinner was as much authorized to believe in Jesus, at first, as at last—that now was the accepted time; now was the day of salvation."[6] This was a tiny crevice of truth, but it pointed the way. To this tiny kernel of truth he clung tenaciously; that a poor sinner was authorized to believe. He had been taught that a sinner could believe, only by the supernatural power of the Spirit. But now, "a poor sinner was capable of belief." That was the cue to his new conception. That was the truth on which the "New Light" Christians built their faith and their evangelism.

At the time he was finishing his college courses, another complication arose: he was aware of a desire to become a preacher of the Gospel. By the orthodox pattern, he must have, for this purpose, some sort of deep spiritual experience with physical demonstration, some dream, a voice from heaven, a vision, or such. He says:

> I made known to my good friend Dr. Caldwell my desire to preach the gospel, but that I had no assurance of being divinely called and sent. He removed my scruples on this subject by assuring me that I had no right to expect a miracle to convince me—and that if I had a hearty desire to glorify God and save sinners by preaching and if my fathers in the ministry should encourage me, I should hesitate no longer.[7]

---

[5] Ibid., pp. 10-11.

[6] Ibid.

[7] Ibid., p. 12.

It would appear that the hand of Providence was leading this earnest, seeking soul, by providing such leaders as David Caldwell and his fellow New Side Presbyterians; William Hodge with his sermon of "the love of God"; Henry Patillo, the revered chairman of the committee to examine the young preachers for their licenses to preach; and Mr. Springer of Washington, Georgia, who understood him so well and encouraged him. The spirit of these encouraging brethren was well expressed by Rev. Henry Patillo when, on approving their tests for license, he handed to each of them, instead of the expected copy of the Westminster Confession, a copy of the Bible, with the admonition, "Go ye into all the world and preach the gospel to every creation."[8]

It was such sympathetic and understanding treatment that enabled Stone to hold on to his determination to preach. It was this understanding spirit, that not every jot and title of the law must be observed, that encouraged him to persevere in his preaching, despite the fact that down in his heart, he was aware that he could not accept the doctrine of conversion presented in the Westminster Confession.

This much of an experience was so much more satisfying than any he had previously felt, that it might have satisfied him—if he had not kept on reading his New Testament. Doubtless many multitudes of penitents had been accepted on as little or even less.

This new idea about how to get faith was making its way in his mind when he was called to be the pastor of the two Presbyterian congregations in Kentucky: Concord and Cane Ridge. He knew that before he could be ordained, and on that occasion, he must submit to questions about his conceptions of the doctrines of the Confession, and must declare his allegiance to the Westminister Confession of Faith. He records his frank procedure:

> Before its [the Presbytery] constitution, I took aside the

---

[8] Ibid., p. 16.

two pillars of it, Doctor James Blythe and Robert Marshall, and made known to them my difficulties and objections. They asked me how far I was willing to receive the confession? I told them, as far as I saw it consistent with the word of God. They concluded that was sufficient. I went into Presbytery, and when the question was proposed, "Do you receive and adopt the Confession of Faith, as containing the system of doctrine taught in the Bible?" I answered aloud, so that the whole congregation might hear "I do, as far as I see it consistent with the word of God." No objection being made, I was ordained.[9]

It is well to observe here, that at the trial of the five brethren before the Synod of Kentucky in 1803, Stone reminded them of his withholding on this occasion, to show that he was not guilty of any breach of promise. It left him free to preach the new doctrine without a break with the Church and without posing as a reformer.

Prior to his ordination, and following it, he was preaching regularly to his two congregations. All this time this battle with the contradiction within the Westminster Confession was still troubling his soul.

Scores of objections would continually roll across my mind against this system. These I imputed to blasphemous suggestions of Satan, and labored to repel them as Satanic temptations, and not honestly to meet them with Scriptural arguments. Often when I was addressing the listening multitudes on the doctrine of total depravity, their inability to believe—and of the necessity of the physical power of God to produce faith; and then persuading the helpless to repent and believe the gospel, my zeal in a moment would be chilled at the contradiction. How can they believe? How can they repent? How can they do impossibilities? How can they be guilty in not doing them? Such thoughts would almost stifle utterance, and were as mountains pressing me down to the shades of death. I tried to rest in the common

---

[9] Ibid., p. 28.

> salve of the day, i.e., the distinction between natural and
> moral ability and inability. The pulpits were continually
> ringing with this doctrine; but to my mind it ceased to be a
> relief; for by whatever name it be called, that inability was
> in the sinner, and therefore he could not believe, nor repent,
> but must be damned. Wearied with the works and doctrines
> of men, and distrustful of their influence, I made the Bible
> my constant companion. I honestly, earnestly, and prayer-
> fully sought for the truth, determined to buy it at the sacri-
> fice of everything else.[10]

During these inner struggles, he was continually at prayer and
Bible reading, struggling in agony of soul to find the explanation
of these puzzling problems of reconciling the creed with the Scriptures.

> During this time, I expressed my feelings to a pious
> person, and rashly remarked, so great was my love for sin-
> ners that had I power, I would save them all. The person
> appeared horror-stricken, and remarked, do you love them
> more than God does? Why then, does he not save them?
> Surely, He has almighty power. I blushed, was confounded
> and silent, and quickly returned to the woods for meditation
> and prayer.[11]

The struggle continued day after day. Gradually he began to
reach some conclusions that appeared to have some sense.

> From reading and meditating upon it, I became con-
> vinced that God did love the whole world, and that a reason
> why he did not save all, was because of their unbelief and
> that the reason they believed not, was not because God did
> not exert his physical, almighty power in them to make
> them believe, but because they neglected, and received not
> his testimony.[12]

Over this text he prayed and read and re-read: "These are writ-

---

[10] Ibid., pp. 29-30.

[11] Ibid., p. 30.

[12] Ibid., p. 31.

ten that ye might believe that Jesus is the Christ the Son of God, and that believing, ye might have life, through his name."

He, himself, recorded the impression that this passage made on his own mind:

> I saw that the requirement to believe on the Son of God was reasonable; because the testimony given was sufficient to produce faith in the sinner; and that invitations and encouragement of the gospel were sufficient, if believed, to lead him to the Saviour, for the promised Spirit, salvation and eternal life. This glimpse of faith—of truth, was the first divine ray of light that ever led my distressed, perplexed mind from the labyrinth of Calvinism and error in which I had so long been bewildered.[13]

Other passages which similarly influenced him are these: Romans 10:17; "Faith cometh by hearing and hearing by the word of God." John 3:16; "That whosoever believeth on him should not perish, but have everlasting life."[14]

He had made the discovery: the key point to the simplification of the process of conversion. The Gospel is the evidence, the mind of man is capable of receiving it, and that is faith. Salvation is the gift of God's grace; not faith—but salvation. Faith is based on testimony which the normal human mind is capable of receiving. The evidence is found abundantly in the New Testament. This was the new conception of faith which gave him the new pattern of conversion; this was the new view which gave to him and to all his brethren the approach to conversion.

At last Stone had reached solid ground. He had found the an-

---

[13] Ibid.

[14] W.G. West, in *Barton W. Stone*, says: "The importance of this moment in Stone's history has not received the recognition which it deserves. Stone's formal departure from Calvinism came when he withdrew from the Synod of Kentucky in 1804. But here, at the very moment he formally accepted Calvinism, he had begun to break with it, by rejecting its conventional pattern of agonizing struggle for immediate commitment to the founder of Christianity." (p. 12.)

swer to the problem. This conception of faith as a normal human process, based on evidence, however much or little aided by the Holy Spirit, was the key to the problem. All the time he was moved by a tender love for his fellowmen, as indicated by the following quotation from his *Autobiography*.

> Had I a friend or a child whom I greatly loved and saw him at the point of drowning, and was utterly unable to help himself, and if I were perfectly able to save him, would I not do it? Would I contradict my love for him, my very nature, if I did not save him? Should I not do wrong in withholding my power? And would not God save all whom he loves?[15]

It was in his later years, while writing his autobiography that he looked back through memory to the dark days preceding this new discovery and penned these lines:

> Let me here speak when I shall be lying under the clods of the grave. Calvinism is among the heaviest clods on Christianity in the world. It is a dark mountain between heaven and earth, and is amongst the most discouraging hindrances to sinners from seeking the kingdom of God, and engenders bondage and gloominess to the saints. Its influence is felt throughout the Christian world, even where it is least suspected. Its first link is total depravity. Yet are there thousands of precious saints in this system.[16]

This, then, was the "experience" of Barton Stone's conversion. It was not orthodox, but it was scriptural; and it was in good conscience—and it was clear and understandable. He could teach it with enthusiasm and clarity. And he did teach it to his fellow "revivalists."

He had been aided in his problem by those blessed "New Side" Presbyterians in North Carolina. Later when he encountered those strict Calvinistic "Old Side" Presbyterians, led by the veteran Da-

---

[15] Ibid., p. 33.
[16] Ibid., p. 32.

vid Rice, he made a clean break with them. Then he was free to teach the Scripture as he read it. And this he did.

This will be recognized, too, as the concept for which, in later generations, Alexander Campbell was accused of denying the existence of the Holy Spirit, and the basis of his criticism against the use of "feeling" in conversion.

Whence and when came Campbell's introduction to this concept of faith?

His biographer, Robert Richardson, answers that query, very plainly. He says:

> During the fall of 1811 and the winter of 1812 he carried on an interesting correspondence with his father upon various topics, among which a large space is allotted to this particular topic. [Faith]
>
> In a sermon delivered on the 7th of April of this year [1811] he thus speaks of faith: . . . "This faith, we are constantly led to understand is of the operation of God and an effect of Almighty power and regenerating grace." (I Jno. 5:1)[17]

This clearly reveals that Campbell's concept of faith was still strongly flavored with Calvinism. Then he began to feel his way along toward, but not yet in, the new concept. This, observe, was in the quiet of his study, not in the agony of personal experience, as with Stone. Richardson continues with his thinking.

> His view of converting faith came to be, therefore, substantially that entertained by J.A. Haldane and John Campbell. It taught him to look to Jesus rather than to trust to the varying moods and emotions of the mind, and upon the merits and faithfulness of Him . . . rather than upon any inward impressions of transient feelings. As a matter of fact, he was not disposed to deny that in many cases a peculiar vividness of conviction and excitement of feeling accom-

---

[17] Robert Richardson, Memoirs of Alexander Campbell (Philadelphia: J. P. Lippincott, 1868-70), I, 413.

panied belief, and under certain circumstances, became unusually striking. Both he and his father had formerly had
such "experiences," as they were called, and he always felt
an interest in the recital of such matters by others, as evidences of their earnestness and sincerity, but he objected
that men were disposed to rely on these rather than on the
Words and Testimony of God.[18]

What a contrast in the "experience" of Campbell and that of
Stone! Campbell's with "peculiar vividness of conviction and ex-
citement of feeling," well within the pattern of Calvinism; while
Stone's, drawn directly from Scriptures, depended on testimony as
the basis of faith, required a clean and final break with the entire
Calvinistic system of evangelism. And this break of Stone with
Calvinism was fully eight years prior to the leisurely correspond-
ence between the father and son on the subject.

It is clear, thus far, from Stone's *Autobiography*, that this conception of faith based on evidence was the first element of the
Reformation that broke into the clear; and it is just as evident that
it was the "New Light" Christian group that brought this new concept into action and inaugurated the Reformation of the Nineteenth
Century.

It is recognizable that this new concept of faith was the very
heart of the evangelizing technique of Walter Scott, which he used
with such power some twenty-seven years later.

How he used this newly-found truth and how he drew his fellow "revival men" into the preaching of it will be the theme of the
next chapter.

---

[18] Ibid., I, 420.

CHAPTER IV
THE NEW CONCEPT OF FAITH PRODUCES SURPRISING RESULTS—INCLUDING THE UNEXPECTED BIRTH OF A NEW CHILD:—A REFORMATION

"From this period [1804], I date the commencement of that reformation which has progressed to this day." B.W. Stone, in the early 1840's.

As we have been able to observe, throughout the series of revivals in America, the ruling motivation was ever the salvation of souls, and the lifting of the morals of the people. This same devoted motivation ruled the heart of Barton W. Stone. Now that he had achieved the assured salvation of his own soul, he had, at the same time, discovered from the Bible, a surer, clearer pattern of evangelism for his vocation as an evangelist. Men could build their faith in Christ by the study of God's Word, and have its assurance of acceptance with the Father, without waiting for an agonizing "experience" at the "mercy seat."

He was eager to put this new concept into practice in his evangelistic preaching. Yet Stone was not a man to jump hastily into any new thing without maturely mastering it. He records his attitude toward this new concept in this way:

> [M]any objections arose in my mind against the new doctrine just received by me, and these objections were multiplied by a correspondent, a Presbyterian preacher to whom I had communicated my views. I resolved not to declare them publicly until I could defend them against successful opposition.[1]

Doubtless he was wise to be cautious. His "experience" was

---

[1] Stone, *Autobiography*, p. 32.

quite new; he sensed that it did not harmonize with Calvinism, although he had come to recognize that some good Calvinists (in North Carolina) were rather broad in their interpretation of the doctrines of the new Confession. Perhaps he pondered and fondly hoped his new concept might come within this wider interpretation.

His "experience" was quite recent. It had occurred after his ordination, which was "in the fall" of 1798, at a time when he still "taught and believed the doctrines" of Calvinism. His "experience" of the new conception of faith must have occurred in 1799 or 1800.

Despite his caution, it is obvious that he did not hold in leash this new message very long, for the next event was the Logan County great revival in the spring of 1801, and he went immediately from there to his own congregation at Cane Ridge,[2] where he preached the new doctrine. His text on that occasion shows that it was the new concept of faith, for it was "He that believeth and is baptized shall be saved; he that believeth not shall be damned."[3] How could he avoid the new concept of faith with that passage for a text? Besides, he says of himself, he "returned with ardent spirits." He was rejoicing in the new concept.

There is much evidence to indicate that the new doctrine was preached during the Cane Ridge revival, the notable revival—in that summer of 1801—some of the criticism against that great meeting was that "Arminianism" and "free grace" were preached that summer. Of course, it may have been some Methodists who preached it, for says Stone:

> The Methodist and Baptist preachers aided us in the work and all appeared cordially united in it, of one mind and one soul, and the salvation of sinners seemed to be the great object of all. We all engaged in singing the same

---

[2] Stone spelled it Caneridge, but from here on, we have adopted the current form of Cane Ridge.

[3] Stone, *Autobiography*, p. 34.

songs of praise—all united in prayers—all preached the same things —free salvation urged upon all by faith and re-pentance.[4]

That last expression sounds like the new idea, "free salvation by faith and repentance." But some besides Methodists were preaching "free grace" that summer. Stone's friend and fellow evangelist Richard McNemar was also preaching it, for the first formal charges were presented against him that very fall.[5] That was only a few months after the Cane Ridge revival.

Of one item we are well assured: that Stone had concluded that the new doctrine "could be defended against successful opposition." Another assured conclusion was that his fellow revivalists had now received the new doctrine with enough assurance to be able to preach it with effectiveness—and despite the opposition of the Presbytery.

In our rush to discuss the implementation of the new doctrine, we have neglected one item of the utmost importance, which fortunately Stone did not neglect in that action-packed summer. Between the Logan County and the Cane Ridge meetings, on July 2, 1801, he went by Muhlenberg and married Elizabeth Campbell, whom he testifies to have been "pious and much engaged in religion."[6] But, of course, that had been pre-arranged. We have previously remarked that events were developing with surprising rapidity.

In all the actions and dealings of these "New Light" brethren, thus far, there was no spirit of defiance. In fact, there is no indication of any intention on their part, to depart from the orthodox pathway. Those mentors of Stone down in North Carolina, the

---

[4] Ibid., p. 35.

[5] McLean, J.P., *A Sketch of the Life and Labors of Richard McNemar* (Charleston, AR: Cobb Publishing, 2014), pp. 16-21.

[6] Ibid., p. 35. (Note: The author of this work mistakenly put the name of Stone's second wife, Celia Brown, in this place. That wedding took place in 1811, after his first wife had passed away.—*Editor*.)

"New Light" Presbyterians, had set the example of using some latitude in their interpretations of the Westminster Confession; it was now a matter of following their example. The Presbytery that ordained Stone had yielded to him the privilege of limiting his acceptance of the Confession to "as far as I see it in harmony with the Bible." He was conscious of this limitation now, and did not fail to remind them of it soon.

Stone and his friends were revivalists; not reformers. They preferred to be orthodox—with room to breathe.

The new truth they were preaching led many to the light. They were convinced they were teaching the Holy Scriptures. They declared they were ready to be judged by the Scripture.

They were conscious of being soul-savers and truth-seekers. They could see no reason why all sincere seekers after truth could not join them in the search.

So far, they gave no indication of any desire to start a reform.

And the general attitude of the day toward the revival was such as to encourage these brethren in their rejoicing at the success of the great revivals.[7]

Let us become better acquainted with these "fellow-evangelists" of Stone, who accepted and used his new doctrine that summer of 1801. The two outstanding, he found in his own neighborhood: Richard McNemar and John Dunlavy. They had received their education for the ministry right there in Cane Ridge under the tutelage of Mr. Robert W. Findlay, the predecessor of Barton Stone, as the local pastor. Mr. Findlay was a man of good native ability, who had received his education m Princeton University (or its predecessor). He had established and conducted the local Seminary after the pattern of the "Log Colleges," as a means of contribution to the supply of preachers, which was running behind the demand for them. Both McNemar and Dunlavy were quite capable, consecrated, and sincere; both had been assigned to pastorates in

---

[7] See C. C. Ware, *B. W .Stone*, pp. 119-120 for examples.

the Washington Presbytery of the Lexington Synod. Both were good friends of Stone and both had become sympathetic with his new concept of evangelism. Obviously, they had preached it with effectiveness that wonderful summer. And no doubt its preaching had made a contribution to the surprising fruitage of that famous revival.[8]

But that undercurrent of hope that the Presbyterians would allow the new doctrine as a part of the latitudinarianism, did not apply to the Kentucky Calvinists as it did in North Carolina.

Various attitudes toward the revival were taken by the several preachers.[9] Among these preachers were some known to be "watchdogs of orthodoxy." These could sniff heresy in the teachings of faith without previous regeneration. The "watch-dogs" began to howl.

The first charge was made against Richard McNemar, in the Washington Presbytery on November 11, 1801. McNemar seems, therefore to have been the more aggressive voice of the five of them, although he was not the leader in seeking truth or in finding it. However, since no person presented himself to substantiate the charges, no action was taken by the Presbytery.

We deem it unessential to carry the reader through all the details of the Cincinnati trials in October, 1802, and the Lexington Synod, September, 1803, where the final break occurred. Both Ware and West have recorded these trials in detail.[10] They are filled with charges, appeals and difficulties. Let us observe Stone's own account of the key portions:

---

[8] Mr. Findlay was a capable scholar and a successful pastor; but he had one fatal weakness: He was discharged from the pastorate on the charge of "habitual inebriety." Custom, in those days, allowed a parson to indulge in the use of intoxicating beverage—but not to excess. The full story of the Cane Ridge Meeting House and of Mr. Findlay is told in James R. Rogers, *The Cane Ridge Meeting House* (Charleston, AR: Cobb Publishing, 2020).

[9] See C.C. Ware, *B. W. Stone*, pp. 119-120 for examples.

[10] Ibid., pp. 125-240; West, *op. cit.*, pp. 47-77, especially pp. 53-57.

In this state of confusion, the friends of the Confession were indignant at us for preaching doctrines so contradictory to it. They determined to arrest our progress and put us down. The Presbytery of Springfield, in Ohio, first took McNemar through their fiery ordeal for preaching these anti-Calvinistic doctrines. From that Presbytery his case came before the Synod of Lexington, Kentucky. That body appeared generally very hostile to our doctrine, and there was much spirited altercation among them. The other four of us well knew what would be our fate, by the decision on McNemar's case; for it was plainly hinted to us, that we would not be forgotten by the Synod. We waited anxiously for the issue, till we plainly saw it would be adverse to him, and consequently to us all.

In a short recess of Synod, we five withdrew to a private garden, where, after prayer for direction, and a free conversation, with a perfect unanimity we drew up a protest against the proceedings of Synod in McNemar's case, and a declaration of our independence, and of our withdrawal from their jurisdiction, but not from their communion. This protest we immediately presented to the Synod, through their Moderator. It was altogether unexpected by them, and produced very unpleasant feelings; and a profound silence for a few minutes ensued.

We retired to a friend's house in town, whither we were quickly followed by a committee of Synod, sent to reclaim us to their standards. We had with them a very friendly conversation, the result of which was, that one of the committee, Matthew Houston, became convinced that the doctrine we preached was true, and soon after united with us.[11]

In harmony with their declaration that they were withdrawing "from their jurisdiction, but not from their communion" they proceeded to organize themselves into a separate Presbytery called "The Springfield Presbytery."[12] This procedure was permissible under the laws of the Church, and had been done before that time

[11] Stone, *Autobiography*, pp. 43-44.
[12] Ibid., p. 45.

and after.[13]

> We wrote a letter to our congregations, informing them
> of what had transpired and promising to them and the world
> a full account of our views of the gospel and the causes of
> our separation from [the] Synod. This book was soon pub-
> lished, called, The Apology [Defense] of the Springfield
> Presbytery. In this book we stated our objections at length
> to the Presbyterian Confession of faith, and against all con-
> fessions and creeds formed by fallible men. We expressed
> our total abandonment of all authoritative creeds, but the
> Bible alone, as the only rule of faith and practice. This
> book produced a great effect in the Christian community.[14]

In the public excitement which followed these events, many
pamphlets were published attacking the revivalists, which "excited
inquiry and conviction in the minds of many, and greatly conduced
to spread our views. The arguments against us were clothed with
such bitter words and hard speeches, that many serious and pious
persons, disgusted and offended with their authors, were driven
from them, and cleaved to us."

The relationship of Pastor Stone with his two congregations
was so cordial that the reader should have the expression of it in
his own words:

> Soon after our separation, I called together my congre-
> gations, and informed them that I could no longer conscien-
> tiously preach to support the Presbyterian church—that my
> labors should henceforth be directed to advance the Re-
> deemer's kingdom, irrespective of party—that I absolved
> them from all obligations in a pecuniary point of view, and

---

[13] When the Old Side and the New Side Presbyterians were contending in
Pennsylvania about the qualifications required for the education of the ministry;
"when it seemed as though a fresh schism would result, it was agreed that each
Presbytery should take whichever course it preferred, and that if a minority
could not conscientiously follow, they should organize a separate Presbytery."
Quoted from W. G. West, *op. cit.*, p. 50.

[14] Stone, *Autobiography*, p. 45.

then in their presence tore up their salary obligation to me, in order to free their minds from all fear of being called upon hereafter for aid. Never had a pastor and churches lived together more harmoniously than we had for about six years. Never have I found a more loving, kind, and orderly people in any country, and never have I felt a more cordial attachment to any others. I told them that I should continue to preach among them, but not in the relation that had previously existed between us. This was truly a day of sorrow, and the impressions of it are indelible.

Thus, to the cause of truth I sacrificed the friendship of two large congregations, and an abundant salary for the support of myself and family. I preferred the truth to the friendship and kindness of my associates in the Presbyterian ministry, who were dear to me, and tenderly united in the bonds of love. I preferred honesty and a good conscience to all these things. Having now no support from the congregations, and having emancipated my slaves, I turned my attention cheerfully, though awkwardly, to labor on my little farm. Though fatigued in body, my mind was happy, and "calm as summer evenings be." I relaxed not in my ministerial labors, preaching almost every night, and often in the day time, to the people around. I had no money to hire laborers, and often on my return home, I found the weeds getting ahead of my corn. I had often to labor at night while others were asleep, to redeem my lost time.[15]

Stone left, as a part of his *Autobiography*, a copy of the main document of this episode of history: *The Last Will and Testament of the Springfield Presbytery*. We are following his example by printing it as a part of the Appendix of this volume. It is recognized as one of the two most important documents of the history of the Restoration Movement. It is couched in whimsical language, but its significance was clear. However, neither diction nor the ideas were pleasing to the stand-pat leaders.

In this atmosphere of antagonism and criticism, the five "reviv-

---

[15] Ibid., p. 46.

al men" gathered on June 28, 1804, in the capacity of the young Springfield Presbytery. It was only the second meeting of that Presbytery, and surprisingly, it turned out to be also its last session. That was not the only surprise of the occasion. A greater surprise was the emergence of a new life— the unexpected birth of a new child, struggling and crying out to be heard.

Like all-natural births, it came from a long line of forbears. Among its ancestors were New Testament Christianity, the Day of Pentecost, the Protestant Reformation, the Act of Toleration of 1693, the Edict of Nantes, the American Bill of Rights, and the American pattern of Christian Revivalism. The more immediate progenitor was the latter, the series of revivals in young America.

The new life was engendered in the passionate struggle between strict Calvinistic theology of conversion and New Testament pattern of conversion.

The progenitors named the new child, "the Christian Church," and commonly referred to it by that title or the alternate, "Churches of Christ." Inasmuch as these names are both Scriptural, they cannot be discarded, so they continue. But at the period of the birth and infancy, the neighbors (as neighbors will) gave it a name indicating some local and temporary association: "The New Lights," prefixed to the name Christian.[16]

Names, indeed all words, grow out of life situations, so they cannot be denied. They may be largely colloquial or they may be relegated to the classification of slang. But that does not deprive them of usage. The name that grows up in history must be used in the studying of history. Hence, in this study the phrase "New Light Christians" is frankly used, but always in quotation marks.

The progenitors of this birth at Cane Ridge on that notable day consisted of a dozen or so dignified Presbyterian ministers assembled in the capacity as the Springfield Presbytery. It was the second meeting of that Presbytery, less than a year old. The fact that

---

[16] For the sources of the name, see Chapter I.

this turned out to be its last meeting makes our figure of a birth more realistic; for this was not the first "mother" to give up a life for a child.

The motivation for its voluntary demise was expressed by Stone:

> Under the name of the Springfield Presbytery we went forward preaching and constituting churches; but we had not worn our name more than a year [actually less than seven months] before we saw it savored of party spirit.[17] . . . [So] in more than ordinary bodily health, growing in strength and size daily, and in perfect soundness and composure of mind ... We will that this body die, be dissolved and sink into union with the body of Christ at large.[18]
>
> With the man-made creeds, we threw it overboard and took the name Christian—the name given to disciples by divine appointment first at Antioch. We published a pamphlet on this name, written by Elder Rice Haggard, who had lately united with us.[19]

We can almost feel the sigh of relief and the prayer of gratitude by preacher Stone, as he expresses himself in these words:

> Having divested ourselves of all-party creeds and party names and trusting alone in God, and the word of his grace, we became a by-word and laughing stock to the sects around; all prophesying our speedy annihilation. Yet, from this period I date the commencement of that reformation, which has progressed to this day. Through much tribulation and opposition, we advanced, and churches and preachers were multiplied.[20]

Thus "a child was born."

Its birthday: June 28, 1804.

---

[17] Ibid., pp. 46-47.

[18] Ibid., p. 47.

[19] Ibid., p. 47.

[20] Ibid.

CHAPTER V
THINNING THE RANKS BY
THE GIDEON'S BAND PROCESS

Stone had recorded in his *Autobiography* the names of "five preachers in the Presbyterian connection, who were of the same strain of preaching, and whose doctrine was different from that taught in the Westminster Confession of Faith of that body."[1] Their names were "Richard McNemar, John Thompson, John Dunlavy, Robert Marshall and myself." When all five of them withdrew from the Synod and then were officially expelled, their adversaries, the stand-patters and the sects, doubtless considered them vanquished. Surely nothing worse than that could happen to them!

But worse did occur. Within six years, Stone had become the only one of the original five remaining as "revivalist" and "reformer." In the prosecution by the Synod, he could see good coming to their Cause: it had cleared up their vision, classified them as heretics, and driven them to become reformers. In this he rejoiced. But what good could he discover in the desertion of the original leaders from their ranks?

The humble spirit of brother Stone seemed to attribute this surprising adversity of theirs to their own sense of pride. For thus he records it:

> But this pride of ours was soon humbled by a very extraordinary incident. Three missionary Shakers from the East came among us—Bates, Mitchum, and Young [in March 1805]. They were eminently qualified for their mission. Their appearance was prepossessing—their dress was plain and neat—they were grave and unassuming at first in their manners—very intelligent and ready in the Scriptures, and of great boldness in their faith.
>
> They informed us that they had heard of us in the East,

---

[1] Stone, *Autobiography*, p. 41.

and greatly rejoiced in the work of God amongst us—that as far as we had gone we were right—but we had not gone far enough into the work—that they were sent by their brethren to teach us the way of God more perfectly, by obedience to which we should be led into perfect holiness.

They seemed to understand all the springs and avenues of the human heart.[2]

After warming up their candidates with these generalities, they finally came down to some specific teachings and demands, which must have made Mr. Stone open his eyes and be on the alert. Stone's account continues:

They urged the people to confess their sins to them, especially the sin of matrimony, and to forsake them all immediately—husbands must forsake their wives and wives their husbands. This was the burden of their testimony. They said they could perform miracles, and related many as done among them. But we never could persuade them to try to work miracles among us.[3]

Strange challenge, wasn't it? Not so remarkable, in that day, as it would seem in ours. For the almost freakish demonstrations of "bodily exercises" of the great revivals were fresh in the minds of the people, and a few decades later, such hoaxes as the Miller promise of the Second Coming had people sitting on the hilltops in companies of hundreds to meet the Lord. Folks were usually more susceptible in that generation, by far, than now. People of the frontier were excitable—and credulous.

Did they win converts to so strange and unlikely an innovation? Verily they did. The more bizarre, the more attractive to some. They played on ambition. Stone's story continues:

Many confessed their sins to them, and forsook the marriage state; among whom were three of our preachers, Matthew Houston, Richard McNemar, and John Dunlavy.

---

[2] Ibid., p. 57.
[3] Ibid.

Several more of our preachers, and pupils, alarmed, fled from us, and joined the different sects around us. The sects triumphed at our distress, and watched for our fall, as Jonah watched for the fall of Nineveh under the shadow of his gourd. But a worm at the root of Jonah's gourd killed it, and deprived him of its shade, and brought on him great distress. So the form of Shakerism was busy at the root of all sects, and brought on them great distress. For multitudes of them, both preachers and common people, also joined the Shakers. Our reproach was rolled away.[4]

It is difficult for us, this far away, to put ourselves in Stone's place, and even imagine what a challenge this situation was to his faith and courage. But some thirty-five years later he could write about it calmly as follows:

Never did I exert myself more than at this time, to save the people from this vortex of ruin. I yielded to no discouragement, but labored night and day, far and near, among the churches where the Shakers went. By this means their influence was happily checked in many places. I labored so hard and constantly, that a profusion of blood ensued. Our broken ranks were once more rallied under the standard of heaven, and were soon lead once more to victory. In answer to constant prayer, the Lord visited us and confirmed us after this severe trial. The cause again revived, and former scenes were renewed.[5]

Then, Stone gives a summary of the Shaker's teachings, as compact and revealing as any to be found, I presume. Here it is, with a digest of their career.

The Shakers now became our bitter enemies, and united with the sects in their opposition to us. They denied the literal resurrection of the body from the grave; they said the resurrection of the body meant the resurrection of Christ's body, meaning the church . . . They, the elders, had con-

---

[4] Ibid., pp. 57-58.
[5] Ibid., p. 58.

stant communication and conversation with angels and all
the departed saints. They looked for no other or better
heaven than that on earth. Their worship, if worthy of the
name, consisted of voluntary dancing together. They lived
together and had all things in common [Socialism or com-
munism], entirely under the direction and control of the elders.[6]

Of course, the pattern of socialism became even more famous
and successful in the Mormon venture, as well as the New Harmony Community of Robert Owen, and many other attempts and
many more failures, which rose and faded during this and succeeding decades in venturesome young America.

Some of those who went into the Shaker ranks must have
found their doctrines to be less than expected, judging by subsequent events:

> John Dunlavy, who had left us and joined them, was a
> man of a penetrating mind, wrote and published much for
> them, and was one of their elders in high repute by them.
> He died in Indiana, raving in desperation for his folly in
> forsaking the truth for an old woman's fables. Richard
> McNemar was, before his death, excluded by the Shakers
> from their society, in a miserable, penniless condition, as I
> am informed by good authority. The reason for his exclu-
> sion, I never heard particularly, but from what was heard it
> appears that he had become convinced of his error. The
> Shakers had a revelation given them to remove him from
> their village, and take him to Lebanon, Ohio, and set him
> down on the street and leave him there in his old age, with-
> out friends or money. Soon after he died. Matthew Houston
> is still alive and continues among them.[7]

This is a sad sequel to the tale, as from this ambitious seeker's
viewpoint. Wouldn't you like to hear the story from the Shaker's
angle? We have it available in J.P. McLean's biography of

---

[6] Ibid.

[7] Ibid., pp. 58-59.

McNemar. Presumably this writer was a friend of the Shakers, for he had high praise for the leaders, and no criticism for their policies.[8]

His story pictures McNemar as the originator and leader of the great Revival in Kentucky, and the leader of the break from the Presbyterians. He admits Stone as having the second of the camp-meetings in Kentucky. The names of the leading elders are recorded, with their power of leadership over the credulous, naive followers.

MacLean's story of the privations of McNemar in his last days of old age is only slightly different from the one Stone had heard and recorded. It seems that customarily the older people, as they became unable to contribute their labors for the good of the "community," were felt as somewhat of a burden. If they had relatives, these were invited to care for them in their homes. Several cases of this kind are mentioned by MacLean, whose account corroborates Stone's as to the dispatching of McNemar to Lebanon, Ohio. McNemar was given a hand printing press which he had personally used for printing pamphlets (he was a skillful printer), in the hope that by its use he could make his living. But, MacLean says,

> Richard had other thoughts; with him he took nothing save that which could supply his immediate wants. Reaching Lebanon he asked the driver to set him out in front of the residence of Judge Francis Dunlavy. The Judge himself responded to the rapping on the door.[9]

Richard requested permission to be a guest in his home until he could communicate with Mt. Lebanon. (Inasmuch as John Dunlavy and Richard McNemar had married sisters, it is assumed that Judge Dunlavy was in the family, somehow.)

---

[8] *A Sketch of the Life and Labors of Richard McNemar* (Charleston, AR: Cobb Publishing, 2014). J.P. MacLean was a universalist minister, but also a historian whose focus was on the Shakers. It appears, based on his works, that he was in sympathy with some of their beliefs.—*Editor.*

[9] MacLean, *McNemar*, p. 88.

There is some indication that the "community" had been taken in by some rivalry in the leadership, between some elders and some "visionists." One elder, Freegift Wells, had taken advantage of Richard McNemar; then they had a sort of public reproachment. Soon afterwards McNemar, as consequence of a hard journey, had a relapse of an old stomach trouble, and died September 15, 1839.

We can scarcely avoid recalling the parallel case of the Mormons in Ohio, who enticed a follower of Alexander Campbell to join forces with them. Undoubtedly, Sidney Rigdon was actuated by ambition for leadership of the Mormons. The same motivation was suspected in the case of McNemar. In both instances these ambitious men proved to be failures. The Mormons succeeded in their economic plans, due to the sagacity of Joseph Smith and his fellow leaders. The Shakers, obviously were not so blessed with sagacious leadership.

Some light may be thrown on the story by citing the report of David Purviance:

> Early in the year 1805 I went to North Carolina and was absent from home nearly two months. During that time the Shakers from New York came into our settlement. Before I came home they were gone to Ohio. I found our people in a commotion; some of my best friends and brethren were much shaken. They represented these Shakers as a very sanctified people, filled with wisdom and godliness. Others believed they were imposters, and were in opposition to them. I hastened to see Stone. They had been at his house; he had examined them calmly and deliberately; he said they spoke with great confidence, that they were assiduous and artful, but he was convinced they were imposters. He said many people had notions that they were possessed of superior wisdom and talent, and that we could not compete with them. But, he said, we must not be afraid of them; — we can confute them. They came among us several times afterwards, but Stone was firm and had fortified me. We withstood them to the face. Some complained that we were intolerant; but being convinced that they were not building

on the sure foundation, we were decisive in our testimony against them both in word and deed. And the churches there sustained very little injury from them.

The case was different in Ohio. Two of our preachers, viz., Richard McNemar and J. Dunlavy were carried off by those seducing spirits, and their congregations much injured. The shock was severe, and our adversaries seemed to expect our entire overthrow. But some good resulted to us from the disaster. McNemar and some others had become somewhat wild and fantastic; their hearts were puffed up before they were caught in the Shaker snare. We took warning to watch and pray, and cleave to the Holy Scriptures, realizing that Jesus was our king and law-giver and abiding in his doctrines, his church would not sink.[10]

It is to be observed that Purviance was living in Ohio, where McNemar was operating, and had opportunity to observe his "puffed up" heart, and his "wild and fantastic" notions better than Stone could have. So Purviance's estimate of the situation was doubtless the wise one. He had had much experience in politics, and was a shrewd observer. It is quite remarkable that these sincere reformers, in that excitable period, came out of this wilderness of temptation unscathed as much they did.

But the Shakers were not the only vexation they were called upon to endure. One other enticement, much more normal, more to be expected, and hence more difficult to withstand, appeared in the guise of the two Presbyterian preachers who stood highest in the esteem of the elders, viz., Robert Marshall and John Thompson. In this instance, they were not dealing with strangers, nor fanatics; these two men were among the best known and most capable Presbyterian preachers in the region. The prestige of Marshall is indicated by the fact that he had been elected, in the Lexington Synod, as the Stated Clerk, for whom they had to select a substitute on the occasion of his withdrawal along with the other four.

---

[10] Purviance, Levi, *Biography of David Purviance* (Dayton: B.F. and G.W. Ells, 1848) [note: page numbers given are from the 1940 reprint] pp. 178-179.

The high standing of Thompson is revealed by a remark by David Purviance:

> In Ohio, Thompson had been the leading preacher, and he was yet beloved and respected among us.[11] I was the only preacher of much experience and age belonging to Christian Church in that country [Ohio]. He [Marshall] commenced sounding retreat and endeavoring to establish the presbyterian system of doctrine. But it was generally remarked that he did not preach with the same life and power as formerly.[12]

We should have the report of this episode from the viewpoint of Barton W. Stone, himself:

> Soon after this shock had passed off [from the defection to the Shakers], and the church was in prosperous, growing condition (for many excrescences had been lopped off from our body), another dark cloud was gathering, and threatened our entire overthrow. But three of the leaders now remained of those that left the Presbyterians, and who had banded together to support the truth—Robert Marshall, John Thompson, and myself. I plainly saw that the two former, Marshall and Thompson, were about to forsake us, and to return to the house from whence they had come, and to draw as many after them as they could. They began to speak privately that the Bible was too latitudinarian for a creed—that there was a necessity, at this time, to embody a few fundamental truths, and to make a permanent and final stand upon them. One of those brethren had written considerably on the points or doctrines to be received, and on those to be rejected by us. He brought the written piece with him to a conference previously appointed, in order to read it to them. It was thought better not to read it at that

---

[11] This was written at a time when the brethren, preachers, were having a consultation at Mount Tabor, Kentucky, about some of the theological problems that were bothering them. These two were trying to persuade the others to accept the use of creeds to hold them within the orthodox lines; the others were hesitating.

[12] Purviance, *op cit.*, p. 156.

time, as too premature, but to postpone it to another appointment, which was made at Mount Tabor, near Lexington, at which a general attendance was required.[13]

In the light of the after history it is obvious that these two men were sincere and earnest, but were not made of the stuff of reformers. They were not able to stand alone on the moving train without holding to the straps. They could not venture out of the beaten pathways; they had to have the support of official creeds to lean on, to feel secure. Stone completes his story:

> Marshall, Thompson and Andrews [another orthodox preacher who had joined them] labored hard to bring us back to the ground from which we had departed, and to form a system of doctrines from which we should not recede. This scheme was almost universally opposed by a large conference of preachers and people. Those brethren, seeing they could effect nothing, bade us farewell, and withdrew from us. Soon afterwards, Marshall and Thompson joined the Presbyterians, receiving their confession again professedly *ex animo*; and charity hopes they did as they professed. They became our most zealous opposers; Marshall was required by the Presbytery to visit all our churches, where he had formerly preached his errors, and then renounce them publicly, and preach to them the pure doctrine.
>
> These two brothers were great and good men. Their memory is dear to me, and their fellowship I hope to enjoy in a better world. Marshall has been dead for some years. He never could regain his former standing, nor the confidence of the people, after he left us. Thompson yet lives [1843] respected, and a zealous preacher of the New School Presbyterians, in Crawfordsville, Indiana. Not long since I had several very friendly interviews with him. Old things appeared to be forgotten by us both, and cast off by brotherly, kind affection. Hugh Andrews joined the Methodists, and long since sleeps in death. Of all the five of us that left

---

[13] Stone, *Autobiography*, pp. 60-61.

the Presbyterians, I only was left, and they sought my life.[14]

Thus purified by the fire of temptation, and refined by the testing of the ability to stand by the aims of the reformation, Stone, with depleted ranks, persevered and prosecuted the reformation, to which he had committed his soul. David Purviance was close by his side, a man of the stuff of reformers. They promptly gathered in recruits, and the Cause continued to prosper.

The principle of reducing forces to the dependable men had triumphed, again, as in the case of Gideon.

---

[14] *Ibid.,* p. 61.

CHAPTER VI
THESE EARNEST EVANGELISTS, DRIVEN TO BECOME REFORMERS, DISCOVER THEIR PLATFORM

These "revival men" had seen no vision from the sky. They had discovered no cryptic message carved on a random stone. They had not planned a reformation. But now, the turn of circumstances had made them into reformers; it was the prosecution of charges by the Synod that drove them to it. In this devotion to the Cause of Evangelism, with the Bible before their eyes, they had encountered certain principles which were true to Scripture and effective in evangelism, and to which they found themselves loyal, even beyond their love for the Presbyterians. To these principles, for the sake of their evangelism, they pledged their loyal devotion. Thereby they found themselves as leaders of a reformation.

What was their platform? They had formulated none. But in the pursuit of their evangelistic efforts, they had practiced those Biblical principles which they were certain were true, and worth preserving; even worth fighting for.

Let us now proceed to trace these principles, somewhat in historical order, as they emerged from their evangelistic labors.

According to the story as we have followed it, the first definite break into the new viewpoint occurred in the "experience" of Barton W. Stone, when by his devoted dependence on the holy Scriptures, he was enabled to perceive that faith was something reasonable. To quote his own words: "From reading and meditating upon it, I became convinced that God did love the world, and that the reason why he did not save all was because of their unbelief; . . . they neglected and received not his testimony, given in his word concerning his Son." Stone saw that "the requirement to believe in the Son of God was reasonable, because the testimony given was sufficient to produce faith in the sinner, and the invitation and encouragement of the gospel were sufficient, if believed, to lead him to the Savior, for the promised Spirit, salvation and eternal life."[1]

May we, now, express this concept in current phraseology, and accept it as the first plank in their reform platform.

FIRST PLANK: Faith is an act of the mind, as well as of the will and the heart; man is capable of receiving and accepting evidence by his normal human senses; the evidence in the Bible is a sufficient basis of faith to make him a Christian. (Negatively, this denies the necessity of a supernatural experience at a specific time and place, as required by Calvinism.)

The fact that this conception of Faith had been preached by McNemar (and by the other evangelists, of course) before November 3, 1801, is obvious from the language of the charges brought against him at that date, as may be observed in the following quotations of those charges.[2]

> 4. He has expressly declared that a sinner has power to believe in Christ at any time;
> 5. That a sinner has as much power to act faith, as to act unbelief; . . .
> 6. He has expressly said, that faith consisted in the creature's persuading himself assuredly that Christ died for him in particular.

Also, less directly, yet in harmony with this concept are these:

> 1. He reprobated the ideas of sinners attempting to pray, or being exhorted thereto, before they were believers in Christ.
> 2. He has condemned those who urge that convictions are necessary, or that prayer is proper in the sinner.

A second principle (or doctrine) they found as their:
SECOND PLANK: Christ died for all men; the grace of God is

---

[1] Stone, *Autobiography,* p. 31.
[2] West, *op. cit.,* p. 55; and Ware, B. W. Stone, p. 127.

free for all who will accept it, or "He has expressly declared at several times that Christ purchased salvation for all the human race without distinction."

For these evangelists to teach this most un-Presbyterian doctrine of "universal atonement," was surely stretching their latitudinarianism pretty far, but it was a part of their determination to follow the Bible rather than any man-made creed. It was really taunting the Presbyterians, who had already become vexed at the Methodists and called them "Arminians" for preaching "free grace." This "free grace" doctrine had grown popular with the American people who treasured their new-found freedom, politically and economically.

The quotation of these charges clearly brings out these first principles of their message. But there is another document which covers much more, since it was devised to defend their stand. We refer to the one outstanding document which these brethren issued in their controversy, *The Last Will and Testament of the Springfield Presbytery*. (See Appendix A for complete text.) It should be borne in mind, however, that this document was not devised for the purpose of expressing their platform of principles as such. Rather, it has limitations in that it was devised for a particular occasion, in the midst of warm controversy, and its language is much affected by these circumstances (which are told elsewhere herein) and at times becomes somewhat whimsical.[3]

The following "Planks," or Principles are gleaned from that document and will be readily recognized by comparing with it:

THIRD PLANK: (Adapted from "Imprimis.") All Christians should be united into the Body of Christ at large, "for there is one body, even as we are called in one hope of our calling."

---

[3] Stone recognized this limitation in his editorial in 1827 (as it is printed in his History of the Christian Church in the West, p. 39), by saying: "The manner in which this piece was written, we confess, did not then meet with our entire approbation, but the matter of it we see no good reason to reject."

It is quite significant that the first principle enunciated in this, the primary document which these men devised, has the plea for Christian unity as its "Imprimis." The fact that this plea was basic with Stone is forcefully enumerated and clearly evidenced by Dr. William G. West in his volume which bears the title, *Barton Warren Stone, Early American Advocate of Christian Unity*.[4]

FOUTH PLANK: (Adapted from first "Item.") That there be one Lord over God's heritage, and his name One," and that name, *Christian*.

It was the presence of Rice Haggard at the meeting on June 28, 1804, that brought this item to a head, no doubt. And the name "Christian Church," which he suggested, and which they adopted on that day, stayed with the group long after the inelegant "New Light" had worn off. The "name of distinction" expressed the spirit of "partyism" and the elimination of that spirit was the motivation for dissolving the Springfield Presbytery.

FIFTH PLANK: (Adapted from the second "Item.") May "our power of making laws for the church and executing them by delegated authority, forever cease."

This, of course, was a renunciation of the authoritative system of churchly courts, Synod, Presbyteries and such, which had restricted the freedom of these evangelists.

SIXTH PLANK: (Adapted from the third "Item.") Let candidates for the Gospel ministry study the Holy Scriptures with fervent prayer and obtain license from God to preach the simple Gospel without any admixture of philosophy, vain deceit, traditions of men, or rudiments of the world.

In view of the restrictive trials through which these men had passed, the implications of this plank are obvious, as applied to

---

[4] This significant book, published by the Disciples of Christ Historical Society in the time of the emergence of the Ecumenical Movement, deserves careful study by all friends of that Cause. It is quite thorough in its highlighting of this plea of Stone.

creeds and church courts. It was a part of their plea for congregational independence, founded on the Bible as the only source of authority.

SEVENTH PLANK: (Adapted from the fourth "Item.") Let the church of Christ resume her native right of internal government—try her candidates for the ministry, and so forth. This was a further plea for local congregational independence and freedom of the preachers from control of higher courts.

EIGHTH PLANK: (Adapted from the fifth "Item.") "Let each particular church, as a body, actuated by the same spirit, choose her own preacher, and support him by free will offering, admit members, and never delegate her right of government to any men or seat of men." Or, declaring for the principle of congregational independence.

NINTH PLANK: (Adapted from the sixth "Item.") We take the Bible as the only sure guide to heaven and the only and all-sufficient rule of faith and practice.

This, of course, is the standard plank of the Protestant creeds, and disregarded, in practice by them all, by their adoption of human creeds.[5]

---

[5] Here let me insert, as apropos, a favorite passage of mine from Schaff, *op. cit.* (VII, 357): "It was a glaring inconsistency that those who had just shaken off the yoke of popery as an intolerable burden, should subject their conscience and intellect to a human creed; in other words, substitute for the old Roman popery a modern Protestant popery. Of course they sincerely believed that they had the infallible Word of God on their side; but they could not claim infallibility in its interpretation. The same inconsistency and intolerance was repeated a hundred years later on a much larger scale in the 'Solemn League and Covenant' of the Scot Presbyterians and English Puritans against popery and prelacy, and sanctioned in 1643 by the Westminster Assembly of Divines which vainly attempted to prescribe a creed, a church polity, and a Directory of worship for these nations. But in those days neither Protestants nor Catholics had any proper conception of religious toleration, much less of religious liberty, as an inalienable right of man. 'The power of the magistrates ends where that of conscience begins.' God alone is the Lord of conscience."

So far, it is easy to recognize several standard Protestant planks in this platform, but more of them with a distinctive note quite familiar to all members of the Restoration Movement. Some of the standards of this movement, though, are missing thus far. However, thus far this story covers only up to 1804. A few years later, additional planks were definitely adopted. We might observe that aside from the topic of baptism, the main points in the "plea" had been observed and adopted by the year 1804.

TENTH PLANK: (Adapted from the seventh "Item.") Let the preachers and people cultivate a spirit of forbearance, pray more, and dispute less.

This was one of spirit rather than of law or rule or doctrine. It was the most characteristic of Stone himself, and had much to do with some of his decisions. Observe the term "forbearance." It was eminently distinctive of Stone's disposition and practice.

Some of us may have wondered what Barton W. Stone thought when he preached that first sermon after his "experience," to the Cane Ridge congregation on the text: "Whosoever believeth and is baptized shall be saved." Doubtless he satisfied his mind by thinking of infant sprinkling as fulfilling the condition of "baptism." In fact, he reveals his development in this field of thought quite freely:

> On this I will state what took place while I was a Presbyterian Preacher. Robert Marshall, one of our company, had then become convinced of the truth of the Baptists' views on this subject, and ceased from the practice of pedobaptism; and it was believed he was on the eve of uniting with the Baptists. Alarmed lest he should join them, I wrote him a lengthy letter on the subject, laboring to convince him of his error. In reply, he wrote me another, in which he so forcibly argued in favor of believers' immersion, and against pedobaptism that my mind was brought so completely to doubt the latter that I ceased the practice entire-

ly.[6]

This could have been as early as 1801, and was certainly prior to 1803, for it was "while [Stone] was a Presbyterian preacher." He baptized no babies after that. His story continues: "But about that time the great excitement commenced, and the subject of baptism was for a while strangely, almost forgotten."[7] Think of it: Stone ceased the practice of infant sprinkling prior to the trials! Perhaps as early as 1801.

And by 1807,[8] they adopted immersion of believers. He continues the passage in his *Autobiography*:

> But after a few years it revived, and many brethren were dissatisfied with their infant sprinkling, among whom I was one.
>
> The elders, brethren and deacons came together on this subject; for we had agreed previously with one another to act in concert, and not to adventure on anything new without advice from one another. At this meeting we took up the matter in a brotherly spirit, and concluded that every brother and sister should act freely, and according to their convictions of right—and that we should cultivate the long neglected grace of forbearance towards each other—they who should be immersed should not despise those who were not, and vice versa.[9]

It is not surprising that Barton Stone had attained and favored an attitude of "forbearance." In his biography of Stone, C.C. Ware has a brilliant page (173) intimating reasons for Stone's conservative and cautious approach "to the problems at this juncture in the development of the Cause." It begins with "Barton Stone has some worries," and climaxes with, "Much trouble was making him wise." The question of the mode of baptism was one which had to

---

[6] Stone, *Autobiography*, p. 55.

[7] Ibid.

[8] James R. Rogers, *Cane Ridge Meeting House*, p. 44.

[9] Stone, *Autobiography*, pp. 55-56.

be faced by these Christians, and Stone was their spokesman. "He must be cautious and conciliatory. He must conserve his movement." In this, Ware sensed the delicacy of the problem facing Stone. The sponsors of immersion, in those days, were the Baptists, who were known to be mostly of the uncultured classes, and their preachers, on the whole, uneducated men, whereas the Presbyterians were of the more cultured class, and their ministers highly educated. Hence, popularly, immersion was not rated as exactly "genteel." And it was from the Presbyterians that the "reformers" could expect many of their recruits. The requirement of immersion could become a barrier to recruiting.

Thus, they were in the same predicament in which Martin Luther had found himself. In his Journal he frankly states:

> As yet I have not desired to make any marked changes in the order of baptism. ... In order not to frighten weak consciences, I allow it to remain quite as it was, in order that they do not complain that I want to institute a new baptism, or criticize those who were baptized in the past as persons not properly baptized.[10]

These new reformers were well aware that the gravitation pull of the christening of babies and family pride and tradition would pull heavily against the requirement of believers' immersion. Hence, not only as a matter of personal belief, but as a strategy for the leadership of the Cause, Stone was driven to a cautious policy, that of forbearance. Observe that this was in 1807, after McNemar, Dunlavy, Worley, and Houston had gone off to the Shakers and Marshall and Thompson were wavering back toward the Presbyterians; Stone was the only original leader left. The situation was shaky; as other preachers joined them, they would look to Stone, naturally, for leadership. Among these new recruits was David Purviance, a former elder in the Cane Ridge congregation, under

---

[10] Martin Luther, Works (Philadelphia: A. J. Holman Co. & the Castle Press, 1932), VI, 206.

Stone's pastorate, whom Stone had recently ordained into the Christian ministry. Naturally he looked to Stone for leadership. He was a man of great personal strength and ability, having served forcefully in the Kentucky State Legislature several terms. He turned out to be the first voice publicly to proclaim in favor of believers' immersion, and the third person to submit to immersion. But he held to the policy of forbearance (and refused to make immersion a requirement) to the end of his life. Others were to be recruited in the leadership, but just at that juncture, Stone (as usual) was looked to for decisions.

In June, 1807, a decision was required. As Ware expressed it: "A young woman at last forced the hand of Stone. She requested immersion."[11] It had already been agreed that they would respect the desires of each individual. But some practical decisions were required to be made. Stone's story continues:

> Now the question arose, who will baptize us? The Baptists would not except we united with them; and there were no elders among us who had been immersed. It was finally concluded among us that if we were authorized to preach, we were authorized to baptize. The work was then commenced, the preachers baptized one another, and crowds came and were also baptized. My congregations very generally submitted to it, and it soon obtained generally, and yet the pulpit was silent on the subject.[12]

This silence of the "pulpit," of course, was due to the policy of "forbearance."

The account of this famous occasion is related in more detail by David Purviance, and is of importance, also on account of his unique attitude toward baptism. David Purviance was the son of a Presbyterian elder who remained faithful to Calvinism and argued it with his son. David relates in much detail his struggle with his

---

[11] Ware, *B.W. Stone*, p. 174.

[12] Stone, Autobiography, p. 56.

inherited pattern of infant baptism and how, step by step, he thought his way through to immersion of believers. When he reached this point, he remarked:

> My conclusion was that had I rightly understood the subject when I was received into the church, I must and would have been initiated by baptism. But I did not realize the obligation or necessity at that time: moreover, as we had experienced many difficulties, and passed through a fire of opposition, I did not wish to incur a new difficulty, or kindle another fire, should it even be done by water. I therefore thought it best to be cautious, and measurably silent on the subject.[13]

Obviously, he and Stone were of the same disposition. But Purviance continues his story:

> Here I rested for a while till a person who had made profession of her faith applied to Brother Stone for baptism by immersion. He appointed a meeting for that purpose at a suitable place [Stoner's Creek near Paris in 1807].
>
> A large congregation assembled. Brother Reuben Dooley attended the meeting and preached a sermon on the occasion. I was there, also.
>
> After the person on whose account the meeting had been appointed, and another woman, were baptized, a man who was a member of the church applied to Brother Stone for baptism.[14]

Evidently, this man was one of many who had been sprinkled in infancy. The account continues that Stone made a short address saying, "I hope the brethren will not be hurt at me, I am going into the water for conscience's sake. Peter said, 'not the putting away of the filth of the flesh but the answer of a good conscience toward God.' I was baptized in infancy, but cannot be satisfied; it is a command of God to be baptized and I cannot have the answer of a

---

[13] Purviance, *op. cit.*, p. 118.

[14] Ibid.

good conscience unless I obey the command." Then came the struggle in the mind and soul of Purviance:

> His words reached my heart. I prayed, like Saul on the road to Damascus, 'Lord, what wilt thou have me do?' Soon after the words spoken by Mary came to my mind, 'What he saith unto you, do it.' I asked myself—what does the Lord say? I soon recollected the answer, 'Repent and be baptized, every one of you, etc.'
>
> I determined to go forward; yet I had a fear of exciting new difficulties or divisions in the church. Our preachers at this time were comparatively few. The Shakers who were associated together had lately made an inroad and carried away McNemar, Dunlavy, and Houston; I knew that the belief of Marshall and Thompson, respecting baptism, was contrary to mine—and I did not know the sentiments of Stone and Dooley, on the subject. I called Stone and Dooley aside, and made known to them in my mind and determination and asked Stone to baptize me—to which he consented. I mentioned that the only thing I regretted was, hurting the brethren. Dooley replied, 'The best way to please the brethren is to please the Lord.' I then addressed the congregation publicly on views on the subject of baptism.[15]

It is well known that this sermon of David Purviance was the first voice in public to come out boldly in favor of immersion as the Scriptural form of baptism, for this group of Christians. In fact he himself wrote a parallel account of this same period which was published in the *Autobiography of Barton W. Stone* by the editor, John Rogers, in which he says, "I then addressed the congregation publicly. It was the first time the subject had been publicly named among us." His story has much human interest; let us follow it:

> We went to the water; before we went in, Dooley said to me quietly, 'As soon as you are baptized, I shall want you to put me under the waters.' Accordingly, as soon as I

---

[15] Ibid., pp. 118-119.

was on my feet, Dooley came forward, and a number more followed, whom I baptized before I came out of the water. Stone was not baptized that day.[16]

Stone reports that his immersion was a little later (out of his policy of "caution and forbearance.") This last fact is verified by Stone's own statement and by Purviance's other account: "Not long after, Stone was baptized."

Their policy of caution seemed to be working well, according to Purviance's testimony:

> None of us urged the matter. We exhorted the people to search the scriptures, and act according to their faith, and to forbear one another in love. Stone studied the peace of the church; and his character for candor and honesty was so well established, that by pursuing a prudent course he preserved the people in unity of the spirit and retained their confidence. In some churches there was opposition, and in some prejudice appeared.[17]

---

[16] Stone, *Autobiography*, p. 118. These items appearing in Stone's Autobiography were inserted therein by the editor, John Rogers, having been written by Bro. David Purviance, at Rogers' request, when the latter was "near fourscore years of age," June 5th, 1843, shortly before his decease on August 19, 1845.

[17] Ibid.

CHAPTER VII
ATTEMPTING TO PRACTICE
THE SPIRIT OF FORBEARANCE

The form of baptism gave Brother Purviance no difficulty. He wrote:

> After I became convinced that believers only were the proper subjects for baptism, I experienced no difficulty respecting the mode, and I think in general the case is similar with others.[1]

The question of the form of baptism did not prove a difficult one for Stone or for those "New Light" Christians in general. They were devoted to the Scriptures as their guide. As soon as they got their authoritative creed out of the way, they quickly realized that immersion was the only form referred to in the New Testament. It did not require the birth of a baby in the immediate family to convince Stone, as it did with Alexander Campbell. Neither did they have to consider throwing in with the Baptists; for Stone's primary objective was Christian unity. To the Baptists was no way to unity; only by following the Scriptures could unity be attained. So when Robert Marshall, writing to Brother Stone, "so forcibly argued in favor of believers' immersion, and against pedobaptism" he records, "my mind was brought so completely to doubt the latter that I ceased to practice entirely."[2] That was before Marshall had begun to turn back to the Presbyterians, hence must have been sometime prior to 1805.

But when it came time to put it into practice, there were some serious complications to be considered: Not a one of the "evangelist" preachers had been immersed; to the vast number of members of their congregations, the question was entirely new. They had all

---

[1] 1. Purviance, *op. cit.*, p. 119.

[2] Stone, *Autobiography*, p. 55.

been sprinkled in infancy, had been through the "experience" at the altar, and were presumably "saved." To consider the idea of being immersed, now, like a fresh convert, was a new, strange conception, and a challenge. "Am I a Christian, or not?" "Have I not been a Christian all these years?"

Moreover, as has already been pointed out, the very act of immersion was unpopular, especially among the Presbyterians. The Baptists were the sponsors of immersion, and in Presbyterian families, immersion was not considered as exactly "elegant." In other words, immersion had an unpopular taint to it, on this frontier. All of this explanation of the social mores can be brushed aside by a few quotations from the New Testament, to be sure. Nevertheless, it was a hard, solid, social fact.

It was out of this situation that the policy of "forbearance" developed.

> The brethren, elders and deacons came together on this subject. For we had agreed previously with one another to act in concert. At this meeting, we took up the matter in a brotherly spirit, and concluded that every brother and sister should act freely, and according to their own conviction of right and that we should cultivate the long-neglected spirit of forbearance toward each other; those who should be immersed should not despise those who were not, and vice versa.[3]

Considering that a small number out of the many were adopting a new, unpopular rite, who could question the wisdom of their caution! That concerned the practice of the form of baptism. The idea of the design came later. Stone tells it:

> The subject of baptism now engaged the attention of the people very generally and some, with myself, began to conclude that it was ordained for the remission of sins, and ought to be administered in the name of Jesus to all believ-

---

[3] Ibid., p. 56.

ing penitents.[4]

He then relates how he preached that doctrine of "baptism for the remission of sins" (Acts 2:38) to a multitude of seekers after salvation, and how it shocked them into confusion. So new, strange, and unpopular was the idea that it was actually distracting to the people. He had told a friend: "It was like ice water thrown on the audience; it chilled them; it came very near driving vital religion out of the church." So Stone resolved to lay aside the theme for a while saying: "Into the spirit of the doctrine, I was never led, until it was revived by Brother Alexander Campbell some years after." (The full story of this will be found on page 56 of his Autobiography.)

When did Brother Campbell revive it? The answer is clear: in the year 1823. He had made a passing reference to it in the Walker Debate, in 1820. But then, it was no more than a hint. He remarked that baptism had some relation to the remission of sins, but the reference was brief and vague. At the early period of the Walker Debate he was much absorbed in the form and the subject (or the person baptized). In the MacCalla Debate in 1823, he began to give serious consideration to the design of baptism.[5]

The time when Stone began to conclude that baptism was "for the remission of sins" must have been in about 1810.[6]

Hence, there was a period of some thirteen years, during which this phase of the subject, i.e. "remission of sins," was not discussed. Since Mr. Campbell's teaching on the subject was what stirred Stone to revive the idea, that must have been after 1823. The subject really became a warm topic of discussion among the

---

[4] Ibid., p. 56.

[5] See Garrison and DeGroot, *op. cit.*, pp. 175-176, where a discussion of this phase may be found. Also in Richardson, *op. cit.*, II, 80ff.

[6] It is mentioned by Stone on pages 56-57 of his *Autobiography*, just after he tells that since Brother Marshall did not have faith in immersion, he (Stone) was called on to immerse some of Marshall's congregation. Marshall went back to the Presbyterians in 1810.

Campbell preachers, only after Walter Scott had made it popular in his meetings in 1827.

During these thirteen years and more of silence on the subject, the "Christian" preachers "were silent on the subject of the form and design of baptism, observing the policy of 'forbearance'." But there was one preacher among them, as already mentioned, who was known to be opposed to baptism as an absolute requirement for fellowship, i.e., "for the remission of sins." That was David Purviance. What were the influences that led him to oppose the position toward which the whole Movement was steadily moving?

For one thing, he had a strong Presbyterian background, and thus the question (which he raised himself) whether he retained any prejudice favorable to his former training. In this connection he concedes that "they are inevitably influenced to believe what they severally are taught. Nothing more or less can be reasonably expected in their infantile state, and thus they had received an early bias which the majority retain through life."[7] That is not to prove bias in this case, only a possibility of it.

There is one observation that might be interpreted in this direction, however. That is, Purviance seems quite easily convinced by some very thin arguments on the question. A few samples will illustrate.

In his Memoirs he declares his full satisfaction with immersion as the true form, then adds: "It seems to be more important for us to ascertain and understand the design of baptism." Then he proceeds for the next 27 pages to present a variety of arguments in detail, against the necessity of immersion as a condition of salvation and fellowship, of which the following is a sample:

> I was pleased with the following expression from one of them very lately: "I should doubt the truth of any doctrine, which would discourage prayer in either saint or sinner." Now it occurs to me that the doctrine that "baptism is

---

[7] Purviance, *op. cit.*, p. 107.

a prerequisite to forgiveness" has this tendency. Every true penitent desires to depart from iniquity. But there may not be a present opportunity for baptism.[8]

This latter "excuse" sounds too much like the old stall of one legalist combatting another, supposing an unlikely calamity: "Suppose a penitent man on his way to the river gets killed by a tree falling on him." At least it is true that many of his points were strained.

Many of the many points of his arguments sound as if they had been hammered over, time and again by legalistic minds.

What would be the attitude toward this question, of the man who proposed and propagated the doctrine of "baptism for the remission of sins," Alexander Campbell? He had occasion, nay necessity, virtually, to answer this question in 1837, in the *Millennial Harbinger*.[9] A casual reference by him to non-immersionist bodies elicited a letter of criticism from a devout lady in Lunenburg, Virginia. In reply he wrote what has come to be known as the famous "Lunenburg Letter." The heart of the reply is contained in these words of his:

> Who is a Christian? I answer, every one that believes in his heart that Jesus of Nazareth is the Messiah, the Son of God; repents of his sins, and obeys him in all things according to the measure of his knowledge of his will. A Perfect man in Christ, or a perfect Christian, is one thing, and "a babe in Christ," as stripling in the faith, or an imperfect Christian, is another. The New Testament recognizes both the perfect and the imperfect man in Christ.[10]

---

[8] Ibid., p. 137.

[9] Millennial Harbinger, 1837, pp. 411f, 414, 506f.

[10] This quotation is from Garrison and DeGroot, *op. cit.*, p. 226f, where also may be found a copy of the famous letter (selections from). Portions of the letter and also of the letter of inquiry, which called it forth are to be found in B.L. Smith's *Alexander Campbell* (St. Louis: Bethany Press, 1930), p. 275. It is well and wise for you to read the entire letter.

Many people will be impressed that Mr. Campbell propagated the duty and significance of immersion much more than he did this broad view expressed in the Lunenburg letter. Naturally, he did so. He was a teacher, inculcating a duty, and an obligation. The broad view was a truth, but not necessarily a pressing duty.

Some people have criticized Campbell, in that he printed this broad view only one time, whereas repeatedly he pressed the obligation of being immersed. It may be remarked in reply, that he took the attitude of the Texas Ranger who was called upon to suppress a riot in a Texas town. When he alighted from the train, a local officer greeted him with, "Did you bring only one ranger?" The ranger replied, "Well, you have only one riot, don't you?" Mr. Campbell had the question asked only one time.

But he did express the broad interpretation: there can be Christians who are not immersed; immersion is not the only condition of salvation. So, Mr. Purviance had a different approach for his broad view. The deep source and the admirable spirit of Purviance's position is well expressed by his son Levi, in his *Biography*, as will be found in the last paragraph of this chapter.

And therein appears another cue to the original question, "Why did Purviance reject the doctrine of 'baptism for the remission of sins'?" One answer is, "because he resented the legalistic arguments and spirit of some of the preachers—followers of Campbell.

This involves another group of "Christians," also—the preachers from another group calling itself the "Christian Church." This phrase, of course, refers to that group who broke off from the Methodists in Virginia (1794) under the leadership of James O'Kelley, and others.[11] O'Kelly never adopted immersion,[12] in fact

---

[11] The author originally had the phrase "Christian Connection" here, but that phrase was not used to describe James O'Kelly's movement. Instead, it was used (spelled "Connexion") by the Christians of New England, in the movement instituted by Abner Jones and later Elias Smith. It is interesting that he does not mention O'Kelly's co-worker, Rice Haggard, by name here.—*Editor.*

[12] O'Kelly's movement split when O'Kelly and William Guirey butted

he was quite antagonistic in his writings against it. Naturally, the Campbell preachers retorted in similar spirit, and having the Bible on their side, they drove home strongly the Bible text on the subject. They also, often and usually neglected the "spirit" of brotherliness. They had no room for "forbearance." Their hard attitude of legalism repulsed such men as Purviance (and Stone), who were pre-eminently of the forbearing spirit. No doubt the harsh legalism of such enthusiasts served to drive Purviance more solidly into his preferred position.

In all of this discussion, the reader should have clearly in mind what was the stubborn nature of the objection to the doctrine of "baptism for the remission of sins." It was much more than a theoretical question concerning the exact point in the process of salvation when the remission occurs; it was whether or not a person who had not been immersed could be considered "saved." It involved the question concerning those multitudes of Presbyterians, sprinkled in infancy, long-time members of the Presbyterian Church, and of exemplary living, whether or not they could be called Christian. In other words, the legalists hotly argued that a person who has not been immersed for the remission of sins, had not had his sins remitted, hence was not a Christian. That phase made the question a very practical one, especially in view of the many Presbyterian friends of the families who had already come into the Christian church, with others of the family and many a friend who had not yielded. Were they Christians?[13]

---

heads of baptism. O'Kelly insisted that sprinkling alone could be considered baptism, while Guirey (with abundant biblical support) stood firm that baptism means immersion—and immersion *only*. The author (Mr. Hall) was apparently unaware of this split, as well as the almost non-existent following of O'Kelly afterwards. He seems to equate the second and third generation "Christian Connexion" preachers (the New England Christians, who generally referred to themselves as "The Christian Church"), who viciously attacked Campbell, with the group associated with James O'Kelly. O'Kelly says nothing in any of his writings that would imply he had any clue who Alexander Campbell was.—*Editor.*

[13] An extreme position along this line is interesting, for comparison's sake.

The difference in opinion on this subject, while not so prominent or serious, did lead to one division of a congregation—one at least. An extract from Purviance's Biography will reveal something of the characteristics of the controversy over the subject of the design of baptism, to show how important it became:

> Although he never believed in the doctrine of baptism for the remission of sins, as published by A. Campbell and others, yet he had all confidence in the honesty and piety of many who did believe in it, and by a cautious and forbearing course, we got along, for the most part in peace and harmony, and rejoiced to believe that we could get along in Christian love, notwithstanding a difference of opinion existed. But in the fall of 1839, by some means, a stranger, by the name of James M'vey was encouraged to preach here [new Paris church]. He was a man of doubtful character, but unknown to the church. He was a peculiar genius, and well calculated to deceive mankind. He commenced a protracted meeting, and continued it until he had got up an extra-ordinary excitement, and baptized near eighty persons, for the remission of sins. He continued visiting this church until he got up an unpleasant spirit, that finally brought about a division in the church that was distressing, and calculated to wound the cause of Christ, and destroy the peace of good brethren. This was very distressing to D. Purviance.

In Texas, in 1858, a new periodical was inaugurated, *The Firm Foundation*, by Austin McGary, for the express purpose of defending and propagating the thesis that unless the person understood at the time of baptism that the purpose of the immersion was for "the remission of sins," there would be no remission, and the person was not a Christian. As is obvious, this position was especially used against the (Southern) Baptists, who claimed that the whole case rested on the "Experience," and baptism was not essential. This story is fully delineated in *The Church on Trial*, by W.K. Homan (Dallas: A.D. Aldridge & Co., 1900); the church at McGregor, Texas, was split wide open over this question. *The Firm Foundation* faction lost out at court, and the progressives retained the building, but the controversy hurt the Cause, severely. Under succeeding editors, *The Firm Foundation* abandoned the public propagation of this belief.

> After this, that once blessed and happy people were known and distinguished by two names, one part was called "the Old Christians," the others "the Reformers, or Campbellites."[14]

We may be sure that this outcome was a great regret and burden to the soul of David Purviance, whose religion was "love" and whose favorite policy was that of "forbearance." After all, our final quotation below from the biographer, Levi Purviance, penetrates more definitely into the reasons for his stiff stand on the disputed phase of the baptism question, than all of his many arguments and all of our surmising.

It is obvious, from our brief contact with Brother Purviance, that he was not a legalist, although he liked to argue. He was not a literalist, though he regarded the Scripture text as final authority. But his interpretation of it was on the spiritual side rather than the literal or legalistic. In fact, his language at times would intimate that he thought some of the brethren arguing for Mr. Campbell's interpretation of this question were altogether too loquacious, too legalistic, and even too stubborn.

We have recorded several quotations from David Purviance. The following quote expresses the heart of his position and reveals the motivations back of it, thoroughly saturated with the spirit of "forbearance."

This is what Levi Purviance says of his father:

> He always stood on, and occupied the same ground that B.W. Stone, himself and others, took more than forty years before—that is, that Christian character should be a test of Christian fellowship. He believed that immersion was the scripture mode and believers the subject of baptism. He was careful to urge baptism as a duty incumbent on all believers. Yet he always kept in view the influence that former teaching had upon his mind; and recollecting that he was once an honest pedobaptist himself, he never could re-

---

[14] Purviance, *op. cit.*, pp. 80-81.

ject from his fellowship those that he believed were honestly serving God; notwithstanding they might differ widely
from him in other particulars.[15]

---

[15] Ibid., p. 81.

CHAPTER VIII
BOTH GROUPS STRIVE REPEATEDLY TO PREACH THE DOCTRINE OF "BAPTISM FOR REMISSION OF SINS"

"Repent and be baptized, every one of you in the name of Jesus Christ for the remission of your sins"—Acts 2:38

The question of the design of baptism was not so easy to answer as that of the form. Yes, immersion is baptism; but what blessing does it bring? Does the forgiveness of sins depend on immersion? Can one be a Christian without immersion?

These questions did not arise at first among these "New Light" Christians, because, in their background, the whole process of conversion was concerned with the Spirit, feelings, and the "experience." They had soon learned, partly to depend on faith rather than feelings, yet they had not gotten away from the atmosphere of the feelings, to depend chiefly on faith. Feelings and other Calvinistic features were still holding back the followers of the Campbell group also, Richardson reminds us.[1]

Even Stone was still held by limitations of depending on feelings; or, at least allowing, and even encouraging the penitents to seek for feelings and depend on them. Yet Stone, all along, sensed the need for something more tangible, and persisted in seeking it. Something was lacking in the customary process. He had found the one item in his "experience:" Faith based on evidence; but that did not satisfy him. It was not tangible enough. The seekers, also, felt the same lack.

Because Barton W. Stone was the earliest of all the reformers in the field of evangelism, he was, also, the first to find and use the doctrine of "baptism for the remission of sins." He used Acts 2:38

---

[1] Richardson, Memoirs of Alexander Campbell, II, 206.

nineteen years before Walter Scott discovered its power in the process of conversion. Barton Stone was the first to mention "baptism for the remission of sins" in an evangelistic sermon, although he did not succeed in getting his hearers to grasp its significance, and had to postpone the use of it for several years.

That episode has been mentioned in the previous chapter but should be told in more detail here. The way Stone brings it in, indicates that it occurred near the time of the notable baptizing occasion at Stoner's Creek in 1807. Let us say not later than 1808.

> The subject of baptism now engaged the attention of the people very generally, and some, with myself, began to conclude that it was ordained for the remission of sins, and ought to be administered in the name of Jesus to all believing penitents. I remember once about this time we had a great meeting at Concord. Mourners were invited every day to collect before the stand, in order for prayers, (this being the custom of the times). The brethren were praying daily for the same people, and none seemed to be comforted. I was considering in my mind, what could be the cause. The words of Peter, at Pentecost, rolled through my mind. 'Repent and be baptized for the remission of sins, and you shall receive the gift of the Holy Ghost.' I thought, were Peter here, he would thus address these mourners. I quickly arose, and addressed them in the same language, and urged them to comply. Into the spirit of the doctrine I was never fully led, until it was revived by Brother Alexander Campbell, some years later.[2]

Of this attempt of his, Stone reported later, "It was like ice-water thrown on the audience; it chilled them."[3] In those days of so much feeling, that was a blow to Brother Stone. He was not in a mood to repeat the experiment. It took him thirteen years to find himself in a position to try it again. And then he does not report it in his *Autobiography*; we learn of it through another, Brother Sam-

---

[2] Stone, Autobiography, p. 56.
[3] Ibid.

uel Rogers. His report is:

> This occurred, I think, in the year 1821. ... I visited
> Kentucky again.... While there, I attended a meeting con-
> ducted by Brother Stone. The interest was very great and
> the audiences very large. Many had professed religion and
> many more who were at the mourners' bench refused to be
> comforted. After laboring with the mourners until a late
> hour of the night, without being able to comfort them,
> Brother Stone arose and thus addressed the audience:
> "Brethren, something must be wrong; we have been labor-
> ing with these mourners earnestly, and they are deeply pen-
> itent; why have they not found relief? We all know that
> God is willing to pardon them and certainly they are anx-
> ious to receive it. The cause must be that we do not preach
> as the Apostles did. On the day of Pentecost, those who
> 'were pierced in their hearts' were promptly told what to do
> for the remission of sins. "And they gladly received the
> word and were baptized; and the same day about three
> thousand were added unto them." He then quoted the com-
> mission, 'He that believeth and is baptized shall be saved.'
>
> When Brother Stone sat down, we were completely
> confounded, and for my part, though I said nothing, I
> thought, our dear old brother is beside himself. The speech
> was a perfect damper upon the meeting. The people knew
> not what to make of it. On a few other occasions Brother
> Stone repeated about the same language, with the same ef-
> fect. At length he concluded that the people were by no
> means prepared for this doctrine, and gave it up.[4]

Meanwhile, circumstances were favoring the breaking through
of the truth, with eager evangelists vigorously striving to teach it
and to stir the people. Others than the preachers were thinking of
the problems, too. Samuel Rogers reports:

> Not long after my return home, there came to my house

---

[4] Samuel Rogers, *Toils and Struggles of the Olden Times: The Autobiog-raphy of Elder Samuel Rogers* (Charleston, AR: Cobb Publishing, 2013), pp. 70-71.

a man by the name of Wentworth Roberts, a very intelligent gentleman,—a school teacher by occupation—who
demanded baptism at my hands. From reading the Scripture
he had come to the conclusion that no one could claim remission of sins without baptism. I asked him if he believed
that the Lord would then and there pardon his sins. He replied that he most certainly did. Said I, "according to your
faith, so be it unto you;" and I baptized him.

Though this was a new doctrine, it made but little impression on my mind; not enough even to set me to investi-
gating the subject. After I immersed him, he came up out of
the water rejoicing; and made a speech at the water's edge,
in which he quoted Peter, (Acts 2:38) "Repent and be baptized, etc." . . . This occurred, I think in 1821.[5]

Another episode with similar connotations is reported by the
same writer, thus:

Brother David Jamison, of the neighborhood of Cane
Ridge had been seeking pardon for a long time, and failing
to get relief, applied to the Word of God for light upon the
subject.

He soon became convinced that a believing penitent
could not claim the promise until he had submitted to baptism. He laid his case before Stone, Dooley, and others,
who held a council in regard to it. Upon due deliberation
they decided that Jamison was a proper subject for baptism—that he had doubtless received pardon, but was not
conscious of it. They baptized him, and he went on his way
rejoicing.[6]

Another case, this time of a preacher in Ohio, continues;

George Shideler[7] had been praying and agonizing for a
long time vainly seeking pardon according to the notions of
our people in that day. One night, about midnight, he came
to the home of Brother Dooley, and, waking him, demand-

_____

[5] Ibid., p. 70.
[6] Ibid., p. 71.
[7] See chapter XIII.

ed of him baptism. He said, he had been seeking pardon for a long time when he had no promises; that from the Word of God he had become satisfied that he had no right to look for pardon until baptized. Dooley baptized him "the same hour of the night," in Seven Mile Creek, above Eaton.[8]

Elder B.F. Hall had an experience similar to that of Brother Stone and tells of it:

> At one of those meetings [in Middle Tennessee or Northern Alabama], in the fall of 1825 an unusually large number were constantly at the anxious seat, weeping and praying, and begging us to pray that God would have mercy on them. Some found relief during the meeting; but the greater number remained uncomforted [at the close, that night]. When the broken hearted mourners came, in a long line, weeping as if their hearts would break, I could sing no longer, but burst forth in a wail of anguish of soul. . . . On the way to the next meeting I said to a brother preacher, "there is a wrong somewhere. Surely, we do not preach as the Apostles and the first evangelists preached."
>
> "Why do you think so?" he asked.
>
> "Because our preaching does not produce the effect theirs did. We nowhere read of persons who were convicted under their preaching going away uncomforted. ..."
>
> I was satisfied that there was something wrong somewhere. This idea haunted me through the whole series of meetings which I attended that fall.[9]

Brother Hall next tells of his discovery of the answer to his puzzle. He relates how, in his journeying, he reached the home of Brother Guess, on Lime Creek. While waiting for Sister Guess to prepare dinner, he browsed for books to read. Fortunately he saw the book, "Debate on Baptism." It was Alexander Campbell's debate with McCalla, in Mason County, Kentucky, in 1823. After reading it he reports:

---

[8] Ibid.

[9] Ibid., pp. 72-73.

I had barely concluded his masterly argument on the subject when I sprang to my feet, dropped the book on the floor, clapped my hands repeatedly and exclaimed "Eureka! Eureka! I have found it!!" And thanks to God, I had found it. I had found the keystone to the arch. It had been lost for a long time; I had never seen it before—strange that I had not. But I had seen the vacant space in the arch a hundred times, and had some idea of the size and shape of it; and when I saw baptism as Mr. Campbell had presented it, I knew it would exactly fit and fill the vacant space. I was now converted over; and was one of the happiest young converts you ever saw.[10]

When Brother Hall tried to pass on to Stone the enthusiasm his discovery had engendered in him, the latter told him of the cold "ice water" reception his own similar suggestion has occasioned in an audience when he had tried to propose just such an idea.[11]

One more occasion B.F. Hall reported that is of special interest because of the person involved.

The next year, in September I think, I preached baptism for the remission of sins on Cypress Creek, in Lauderdale County, Alabama, on Lord's Day night. Talbert Fanning was present and heard the discourse, was convinced of the truth, and, when the invitation was given came forward and made the good confession and was immersed the next morning for the remission of sins. Brother James E. Matthews embraced the sentiment, at or soon after the time, and at my instance wrote several articles on the subject, addressed to Brother B.W. Stone, which were afterward published in his Christian Messenger.[12]

This makes two occasions when Brother Stone tried to preach the doctrine of "baptism for the remission of sins" and failed. The

---

[10] Ibid., pp. 73-74.

[11] See our account of the incident earlier in this work, taken from Samuel Rogers, *op. cit.*, pp. 70-71.

[12] S. Rogers, *op. cit.*, pp. 74-75.

first was in 1808; the second in 1821. We must recall, also, the language of Brother Samuel Rogers: "On a few other occasions Stone repeated about the same language with the same effect." So it is at least three times for Stone.

Mr. Campbell, of course, included the theme in his debate with McCalla in 1823. But this pronouncement seems not to have awakened any wide-spread interest in the idea. The printed report of the debate was probably beginning to stir some interest in it, as shown in the experience of Dr. B.F. Hall, which has just been cited. But judging from the discouraged attitude of Brother Stone, in 1826, as just mentioned, it seems that he had not read of the debate. We know, however, that the influence of Campbell's debate was beginning to permeate Kentucky, for it helped to win "Raccoon" John Smith. Of one thing we are sure, however; it was not yet applied in evangelism.

And Mr. Campbell did not work it out by himself. Fortunately Dr. Richardson was closely associated with the preachers at the Campbell headquarters and could learn of the detailed occurrences among the several preachers in that group. Alexander Campbell had proposed Walter Scott as the evangelist for the Mahoning Association in 1827, but did not do any suggesting to Scott as to the messages he should preach in the evangelizing. This fact becomes obvious from the following narrative which Dr. Richardson records in his Memoirs of Alexander Campbell. This is an unusually long quotation, but we believe its importance will justify its length. The preliminary remarks of Dr. Richardson are especially enlightening, revealing as they do, the remains of the Calvinistic doctrine in the minds of the Campbell group and region. The Kentucky people were not alone in harboring the influences of the out-worn system. And the slight comprehension of the place of baptism among the people of that northern region is somewhat surprising. Stone was not the only teacher who was having difficulty in arousing the people to a new approach to the problems of conversion. The report of Dr. Richardson runs as follows:

This was, in view of all the circumstances, a very difficult and perplexing question. Calvinistic views still lingered to a large extent among the Mahoning churches. Election, effectual calling, theories of regeneration, still occupied the minds of many. Various satisfactory evidences of a true faith were still required before admission to baptism, which was looked upon as a means of admission into the church—a command to be obeyed by those who were already converted. No special promises were recognized as connected with it, and it was very unusual to hear this subject presented at all, except when someone was about to be baptized. Mr. Scott, Elder Bentley and some others of the prominent preachers, were indeed aware that Mr. Campbell had spoken of it at the McCalla debate as a pledge of pardon, but in this point of view it was, as yet, contemplated only theoretically, none of them having so understood it when they were themselves baptized, and being yet unable properly and practically to realize or appreciate its importance in this respect. Hence, almost from the first moment of his appointment, Mr. Scott's mind was thrown into a state of great perplexity amidst the discordant and confused views relating to conversion. Baptism still seemed to present itself as in some way intimately connected with the personal enjoyment of the blessings of the gospel, but he was unable as yet to perceive the exact position which it occupied in relation to other requirements.

About this time, Adamson Bentley went down to Braceville, with Jacob Osborne, to hold a meeting. In a discourse which he delivered on the occasion he was led to speak of baptism, and gave the views which Mr. Campbell had presented in the McCalla debate, affirming that it was designed to be a pledge of remission of sins. While they were on their way back to Warren, after the meeting, Jacob Osborne said, "Well, Brother Bentley, you have christened baptism today."

"How so?" said Mr. Bentley.

"You termed it a remitting institution."

"Well," rejoined Mr. Bentley, "I do not see how this conclusion is to be avoided with the Scriptures before us."

"It is the truth," said Mr. Osborne, who was a great student of the Bible; "and I have for some time thought that the waters of baptism must stand in the same position to us that the blood of sacrifices did to the Jews. 'The blood of bulls and of goats could never take away sins,' as Paul declares, yet when offered at the altar by the sinner he had the divine assurance that his sin was forgiven him. This blood was merely typical of the blood of Christ, the true sin-offering to which it pointed prospectively, and it seems to me that the water in baptism, which has no power in itself to wash away sins, now refers retrospectively to the purifying power of the blood of the Lamb of God."

Soon afterward, meeting with Mr. Scott, they all three went down to Howland, and the discourse at Braceville and subsequent conversation being brought up, Mr. Scott fully coincided in the views expressed. In one of his discourses at Howland, Mr. Osborne again introduced the subject, and proceeded to say further that no one had the promise of the Holy Spirit until after baptism. This remark seemed to strike Mr. Scott with surprise, and after the meeting he said to Mr. Osborne, "You are a man of great courage"; and turning to Mr. Bentley, he added: "Do you not think so, Brother Bentley."

"Why?" said Mr. Bentley.

"Because," said he, "he ventured to assert today that no one had a right to expect the Holy Spirit until after baptism."

From this moment, Mr. Scott's mind seemed to be engrossed with the consideration of the consecutive order appropriate to the various times in the gospel, he proceeded to place them thus: 1. faith; 2. repentance; 3. baptism; 4. remission of sins; 5. Holy Spirit. This view relieved at once his previous perplexities, and the gospel, with its items thus regularly disposed, seemed to him almost like a new revelation. He felt that he had now obtained a clue which would extricate men's minds from the labyrinth in which they were involved in relation to conversion, and enable him to present the gospel in all its original simplicity.

While meditating on these things, and debating with his

own irresolution in regard to their presentation to the public, he met with Joseph Gaston, [a "New Light" preacher]
to whom he freely communicated his thoughts, and who,
delighted with the new view of the gospel thus given, at
once declared it to be the truth, and that it ought to be
preached to the world.

Thus encouraged, Mr. Scott determined to make the experiment; but fearing to give cause of offense to the
churches who had employed him, he set an appointment
outside of the Association ground, and with considerable
trepidation, but in an earnest and interesting manner, laid
before the audience his analysis of the gospel, and at the
close gave a formal invitation to any so disposed to come
forward and be baptized for the remission of sins. No one,
however, came. The effort was a failure. He accordingly
gave notice that he would deliver in New Lisbon a series of
discourses upon the Ancient Gospel.

At the time appointed there was a considerable audience, and the novel manner in which the speaker introduced
his theme, along with his own obvious, intense engaged-
ness and excitement, created no little interest and expectation. His discourse was based upon Peter's confession,
Matt. 16:16, in connection with the same apostle's answer
to the inquiry, "What shall we do?" given to the penitents
on the day of Pentecost, Acts 2:38. As the lordship and glo-
ry of Christ, the Son of God, was his favorite theme, and he
was, on this occasion, animated with more than usual fer-
vor, he became most eloquent, and held the audience in a
state of rapt attention as he gradually developed the power
of the simple but comprehensive Christian creed—the rock
which Christ announced as the foundation on which he
would build his Church; the grand proposition proved by
the miracles of fulfilled prophecy, supernatural wisdom,
divine love, healing power and victory over the grave, detailed by the evangelists, that men might believe, and, "believing, have life through his name."

And when he went on to show how this gospel was ad-
ministered in the beginning, and that believers were baptized into the name and into the death of Christ, and being

thus buried with him and raised again to a new life, received in this symbolic act the remission of sins and the promised Holy Spirit, which was the seal of the Christian covenant and the earnest hope of an eternal inheritance, his hearers, while charmed with such a novel view of the simplicity and completeness of the gospel, were, as on the former occasion, filled with doubt and wonder and were ready to ask each other, "How can these things be?"

Just as he was about closing his long discourse, and while he was exhorting the people to rest in the word of God in preference to all human systems of religion, a stranger entered the assembly, and when, a few moments afterward, the speaker closed by again quoting Peter's words and inviting any present to come forward and be baptized for the remission of sins, this stranger, to the surprise of all, at once stepped forward and presented himself. Here was a singular circumstance. This person had not been enlightened and convinced by the preacher, for he had heard only his few closing remarks. Yet he came forward with all the firmness of an assured purpose, and all the tokens, of intelligent apprehension, to request baptism for the remission of sins!

Mr. Scott knew not what to think of it. The individual, when carefully questioned, seemed perfectly to understand the matter, just as did the preacher himself. There being, therefore, no reason for delay, Mr. Scott, taking the confession of the candidate, baptized him in presence of a large concourse "for the remission of sins," thus annexing to the usual formula the words of Peter, Acts 2:38, explanatory of the purpose of the institution. The people were filled with bewilderment at the strange truths brought to their ears, and now exemplified before their eyes in the baptism of a penitent for a purpose which now, on the 18th of November, 1827, for the first time since the primitive ages was fully and practically realized.

A great excitement at once ensued; the subject was discussed everywhere through the town, and Mr. Scott, continuing daily to address increasing audiences and developing his views of the gospel in all parts, succeeded, before

the close of the meeting, in inducing in all seventeen persons to accept the primitive faith and baptism. Thus, the
charm was broken; the word of God had triumphed, and the
veil which theology had cast over men's hearts was re-
moved. Henceforth the Reformation, which had already re-
stored to the Church the ancient order of things and the
simplicity of the primitive faith, was enabled to make a
practical application of the gospel to the conversion of the
world.[13]

In view of our recital of Stone's two failures at preaching "baptism for the remission of sins," it is interesting to observe Richardson's comment on Scott's similar experience:

It remained, however, still a mystery that his (Scott's)
first two discourses should have failed to convince anyone,
and that at the close of the second, an individual who had
heard neither of them should have come forward intelli-
gently with little more than a simple invitation. In order to
clear up the matter, he thought best after some time to address a letter to the individual, requesting him to explain
the reason which had induced him to present himself.[14]

The reply came from Mr. Wm. Amends, explaining that he had
been a close student of the Scriptures; had become dissatisfied with
the old Calvinistic doctrines which required a mystical experience;
had read the story of Pentecost, in Acts, the second chapter. Then
he had told his wife:

Oh, that I could hear the gospel in these same words as
Peter preached it. I hope I shall some day hear it, and the
first man I meet, one who will preach the gospel thus, with
him will I go. So my brother, the day you saw me come into the meetinghouse, my heart was open to receive the
word of God.[15]

---

[13] Richardson, *Memoirs of A. Campbell*, II, 206-212.

[14] Ibid., II, 213.

[15] Ibid., II, 214.

The author of this book is happy to testify that his own father, Robert M. Hall had exactly the same experience. Having been reared a Baptist, and repeatedly failing of the mourner's bench experience, and studying the New Testament closely, made much the same promise, as Mr. Amends—and fulfilled it; he was immersed by preacher Levi McCash, in about 1885. Indeed, in that generation, that was not such a rare experience.

When Stone got the idea mastered and proved by practice in preaching, he was zealous in propagating it, for instance, through the *Christian Messenger*. This is evidenced by a reply he printed in his journal in reply to a query from "J.E. Church, a Christian preacher, bearing the date New Lisbon, Ohio, July 26, 1828." He refers to the "method and manner" of Walter Scott's recent evangelizing, and asks for Brother Stone's views on the subject. Stone's reply is:

> You wish me to give my views on the manner of Brother Scott's baptizing the believing subject prior to the remission of sins, and of his receiving the Holy Spirit. I am sorry that I have not the back numbers of the Messenger to send you, in which this subject is particularly treated. We have for some time since practiced this throughout the country. Many of the most successful Baptists pursue the same course. I have no doubt that it will become the universal practice, though vehemently opposed.[16]

This is the ragged, rugged story of the slow, struggling emergence of the doctrine of "baptism for the remission of sins," which, after it came into use, made such a marvelous contribution to the success of evangelism in the Restoration Movement. The development of it went through both groups of reformers, each side contributing a share in its emergence; both groups utilizing it as they merged into one body. It started with Brother Stone, who tried it again and again, debated by Brother Campbell but not used by him

---

[16] *The Christian Messenger*, VI, 262, quoted by Ware, *B.W. Stone*.

in evangelism; used by other "New Light" evangelists on several occasions, including Elder B.F. Hall; and finally worked out under successive trials by several evangelists, including three of the Campbell group and one Stone disciple; glorified by usefulness in the merging brotherhoods working as one.

Of course, Walter Scott is the evangelist who received, claimed, and earned credit for "restoring the ancient gospel" by popularizing the famous steps of conversion as stated in his well-known "five finger exercise: faith, repentance, baptism, remission of sins, and the gift of the Holy Spirit." But he was not alone in the process. Once again it would seem that "the truth and the Lord did the spreading."

CHAPTER IX
THE TRUTH AND THE
LORD DO THE SPREADING

"If ye continue in my word, you are my disciples, and you will know the truth, and the truth will make you free." Jno. 8:31, 32

The coming to life on June 28, 1804, of the new child—a Reformation—was unplanned; nobody was more surprised than its progenitors. Their attention and program were all concentrated on evangelism—the winning of souls from sin to salvation. No human mind had devised a platform of reform, nor projected a campaign. Like a human waif this one came into the world sans parents or plans, except favoring conditions and a generous Providence.

Those of us who endeavor to comprehend the forces that engendered it, and guided it to success, must not overlook the psychology of the generation into which this child was born. It was one of great excitement! Emotionalism was dominant, among the people. This was more dominant even than the state of confusion over theology and the rivalry of creeds and parties. This is evidenced by the marvelous camp-meetings that marked the period as unique and climactic. Also, by the temporary success of the fanatical Shaker Movement, at that very moment. Some mighty Providence divine must have been operating above these human scenes that order came so successfully out of such chaos, with such meager human means available.

Yet, as Stone looked back on it from his later years, he could record the story with optimism. "The churches and preachers grew and were multiplied." Then, grateful as he was for this progress, he confessed his fault in the next development: "We began to be puffed up at our prosperity. . . . But this pride of ours was soon humbled by a very extraordinary incident." Then follows the story of the inroad by the Shakers, climaxed in the next four years by the defection of Marshall and Thompson back to the creedism. So that the year 1810 was the nadir.

Of the original five "evangelists" only Stone was left faithful.

It would be a poor, spiritless literalist, however, who would count Barton W. Stone as alone in 1810. This was a Cause that called for a prophet! Not a mere predicter, not a calculates but a seer. And this he saw, through the same medium on which he had depended, all along—the divine Word of God, the Bible. By this he charted the way. And that meant by praying with the Bible open before him. That meant, also, enlisting young men to study the Word, and preach it, along with him. It was the truth in the Word on which he leaned. And it was the loving Father above who watched over the young child, the Reformation—to protect it from its attackers and guide it on its way.

As we look back to the beginning of their independency, we discover that Providence went before them. Some surprising recruits were in their midst on that notable June 28th, 1804, when their declaration of release had been written down and emblazoned to the world, although somewhat crudely cast, in the *Last Will and Testament*. Three sojourners from Virginia were unexpectedly present that day, and they proved to be kindred spirits.

Stone records in his *History of the Christian Church in the West*, immediately following the break in the Synod, in 1804:

> The business was therefore indefinitely postponed, and we returned to our respective homes.
>
> Three valuable Elders, who had a few years before separated with James O'Kelly from the Methodist connection, about this time united with us. Their names were Clement Nance, James Read, and Rice Haggard, the latter of whom soon after published a pamphlet on the name Christian, proving that by this name alone every member of Christ's body should be called.[1]

---

[1] Stone, *History of the Christian Church in the West*, p. 42.

Ten years before, Haggard had thrown out a surprising challenge to a group of possible reformers at a meeting of "Republican Methodists" who had broken away from the autocratic control of Bishop Francis Asbury and adopted that patriotic name. (This was the origin of the Movement under James O'Kelly and Rice Haggard.) In their meeting in Surry County, Virginia, he held a copy of the New Testament in his hand and said, "Brethren, this is a sufficient rule of the faith and practice, and by it we are told that the disciples were called Christians, and I move that henceforth and forever the followers of Christ be known as Christians simply."[2]

This suggestion came at the right moment in the Cane Ridge gathering on that day; it was heartily adopted by this group who had already freed themselves from creedal and ecclesiastical control.

It was a bold step forward; they were ready for that step, and they took it with zeal. Henceforth they were to be known as "Christians" and the group as the "Christian Church."

Thus, they had, Providentially, not only three capable evangelists added to their preaching force, but added to their basic principles—a name.

One of these three, Clement Nance (1756-1828), after a few years, moved on with the tide of migration to Indiana, where he became a valuable evangelist. This was not a loss; it was rather the establishment of an additional out-post, beyond the border.

The outstanding man of this Virginia trio, however, was Rice Haggard, who is named by every recorder of the period as the man who proposed the name "Christian." His brother, David Haggard, was probably just as strong a personality and preacher, although Rice is better known on account of his notable proposal. David had settled in Cumberland County, Kentucky, several years previous to

---

[2] Hall, Colby D., in Cobb, Bradley S., editor: *Forgotten Soldier of the Restoration: The Life and Writing of Rice Haggard* (Charleston, AR: Cobb Publishing, 2020), p. 40.

his brother. Both of them made their homes in Burkesville, Cumberland County, had helped to establish the Christian Church there, and evangelized throughout Southern Kentucky. Indeed, Rice was one of those who travelled into Ohio, also, evangelizing. It was on a trip combining business and evangelism that he died in Ohio, in 1819.

Thus, in a very few years, three states had out-posts of evangelizing engaged in behalf of the Cause. It may well be observed here, that Illinois and Missouri became strongly fortified by preaching brethren soon, and at length.

But directly out from old Cane Ridge the evangelizing was pouring, despite the necessity of Stone's removal of his home from the old congregations.

In reckoning the forces on which the new reformation could count on its side for the coming struggle, we must not overlook the faithful congregations, Cane Ridge and Concord. The tender relationship that existed between pastor Stone and his people, and the loyalty they had for their officially ousted minister.

One item obviously needed was the enlistment of additional preachers to proclaim the truth. New voices must be raised up to take the places of those who had left, as well as many new ones besides. Between the lines a policy crops out which was the answer to this need. Brother Samuel Rogers expresses it incidentally in his Biography:

> In those pioneer times among the converts, it was customary for almost all of them to take some part in the social meetings that were held from house to house, among the brethren. Not only did most of the young men pray, and sometimes exhort, and relate their experiences, but some of the women prayed, and sometimes exhorted with great warmth.[3]

This policy of encouraging self-expression by the young men

---

[3] Samuel Rogers, *Autobiography*, p. 36.

of the congregation must have been going on as a part of his pastoral teaching, for it had yielded fruitage early. One brother in the Cane Ridge congregation, a man of superior abilities and training, had already attained distinction as a citizen has been recorded,

and a politician through his services as a member of the Kentucky State Legislature. His name was David Purviance; he was an elder in the Presbyterian congregation as early as 1799. Stone had encouraged him in preaching and in 1803 led in ordaining him to the ministry. He added much to the strength of the local and general ministry, later becoming the recognized leader of the Christian Church of Preble County, Ohio. His story is told in this volume, Ch. XIII. Other younger preachers developed as the months went by.

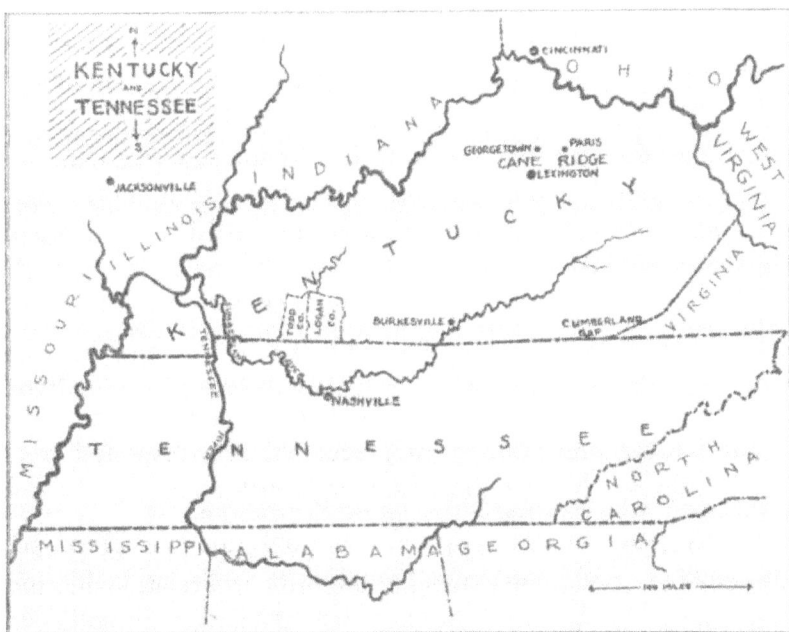

There were other preaching recruits from the Cane Ridge congregation. Samuel Rogers, after a boyhood period on the Missouri frontier with the family, had settled in the Cane Ridge community and "under the preaching of Stone and R. Dooley became a firm believer in Christianity, was convicted of sin and immersed in

Hingston Creek"[4] soon after 1812, after his service as a soldier in the war. He knew the language of frontiersmen better than of books; but he knew the story of the Christ and his church thoroughly and was wonderfully successful in spreading the new Gospel. His final record shows him to have been one of the best recruiters among them.

The evangelist who made the final move in winning Rogers, too, is numbered among the "reapers" of the harvest. Reuben Dooley was another earnest and capable preacher of the Word, of frontier pattern, with the limited schooling of the frontier, but with the touch and language of the people.

Samuel Rogers gives this account of the evangelist who was the agent in his own conversion:

> About this time [1814 perhaps], there appeared amongst us a most remarkable character, in the person of Reuben Dooley, from the settlement of Barren County, Kentucky. Reuben Dooley was considerably my senior, a man of great physical endurance, plain in attire, and, in his address, humble as a child; but zealous, prayerful, hopeful and untiring in his labor of love. His forte, as a preacher, was chiefly in exhortation. . . . Hundreds were again rallied to the standard of the Prince of Peace, and hundreds converted to Christ. . . . Under the searching appeals of this wonderful man of God, my heart was again melted, and from that day to the present year of grace, 1870, I, myself, have been humbly striving to call sinners to repentance.[5]

This quotation opens up to us, not only the tone of the personalities of these two preachers but the brotherly relationship that existed among them generally. The life of Dooley is related in our Chapter XIII.

Reuben Dooley became a very close companion to Barton Stone. They teamed up on many an evangelistic tour. They had

---

[4] Ibid., p. 31
[5] Ibid., pp. 35-36.

common interests. Both of them for a while were widowers, both with little children whom they were boarding out. As they travelled together, they agreed that this situation was unsatisfactory; they resolved each to seek a suitable wife, soon. Stone found his in Celia Bowen, a cousin of his first wife, October 11, 1811. Dooley found his at Cane Ridge a few months later.

The vigor of their travelling-preaching throbs through the story of Stone's *Autobiography*. For instance:

> I had an appointment of long standing in Meigs County, Ohio, above the mouth of the Kenhaway, in order to preach and to baptize a Presbyterian preacher, living there, whose name was William Caldwell. The time drew near and I had no money to bear expenses. I was ashamed to beg, and unable to obtain it. The night before I started on my tour, I had a meeting in the neighborhood, and when the people were dismissed, a letter was slipped into the hands of my little daughter by some unknown person. She handed it to me and I found a ten-dollar bill enfolded, with these words, only, written: "For Christ's sake." I was much affected, and received it thankfully from the Lord to enable me to do his work.[6]

After immersing the Presbyterian in the "Ohio river," he attended a gathering of "separate Baptists," who invited him to speak to them, and to advise with them, concerning a difficult case of dissension they had under consideration. He says:

> I exerted myself with meekness against sectarianism, formularies and creeds, and labored to establish the scriptural union of Christians and their scriptural name. . . .
>
> The mind of the association was withdrawn from any farther attention to their knotty case, to the consideration of what I had said. The result was that they agreed to cast away their formularies and creeds, and take the Bible alone for their rule of faith and practice—to throw away the name

---

[6] Stone, *Autobiography*, p. 65.

Baptist, and take the name Christian—and to bury their association and to become one with us in the great work of Christian union.[7]

This sample of his story is characteristic of many like it and of the spirit of the evangelist with the response. It reveals very well how these sincere preachers of a great message could start from a small beginning and beat the pathway for a great crusade for Christian faith and unity. Thus, is the heading of this chapter illustrated and justified: "The truth and the Lord do the spreading."

We, seemingly, have been following the example of these frontier proclaimers, by appearing wherever the Spirit leads us. A few sample quotations, therefore, from Stone will be in harmony:

> We preached and baptized daily in Eaton [Ohio, Preble County] for many days. No house could contain the people who flocked to hear. We had to preach in the open streets to the anxious multitude. At night, after service, the cries and prayers of the distressed in many houses around, were truly solemn. Almost the whole town and neighborhood were baptized and added to the Lord.[8]

Stone records his and Dooley's travels: "We preached and founded churches throughout the Western states of Ohio, Kentucky, and Tennessee."[9]

The mention of Ohio is interesting. We usually think of that as a region covered by the Campbells and Scott. Indeed, the Mahoning Baptist Association was their special area of operation. That was a northern tier of about a dozen counties along Lake Erie near Pennsylvania.[10]

But the evangelists of the Christians of the Stone variety had

---

[7] Ibid., pp. 65-66.

[8] Ibid., p 67.

[9] Ibid., p. 62.

[10] For a discussion of the Western Reserve, see A.S. Hayden, *Early History of the Disciples in the Western Reserve, Ohio* (Cincinnati: Chase and Hall, 1875), p. 13ff.

some rather strong communities in several of the counties and regions farther south in the state. These, of course, were out-posts of the colonies in Kentucky. Kentucky was the pioneer state west of the mountains, admitted to the Union in 1792, whereas Ohio came in eleven years later. The tide of immigration had poured into Kentucky, through the Cumberland Gap, through Virginia and Carolina before the territory was opened up for settlement in Ohio.[11]

One of the earliest moves from the south into Ohio, was that made by David Purviance, in 1807. The conversion of the Presbyterian and the separate Baptists by Stone, as told a few pages back, are only samples of the recruiting accomplished by him and others. From Preble County came several preachers of the Reformation, of the "Christian" variety, whose stories are related in Chapter XIII. Some of these are Thomas B. Kyle, George Shideler, John Hardy, William Dyer, and Thomas Adams. They are worth studying, as types.

The narratives of Stone's evangelizing during the years after 1810 give us an idea of his concentration on his mission of planting the Cause in several states, despite the remark of one historian that he had to spend most of his time "making a living." To the latter task, he was compelled to devote much of his strength, to be sure. His personal and family moves have been so meticulously traced out and recorded by C. C. Ware[12] that it would be superfluous to detail them here and aside from the present purpose. What is more to our theme is the number of churches planted, multitude evangelized and preachers enlisted, in the crusade of the "Christian Church" forces.

After the fusion of the two Movements, the distinction between the leaders of the one side and the other, happily, came to be more unobserved. But for the sake of history we are obliged to record

---

[11] The historical setting of this is told in Hall's contribution to *Forgotten Soldier of the Restoration*, .pp. 46-47.

[12]. *Barton W. Stone*, Chapters XIII-XV.

here the names of many of the evangelists who were won and largely led by the preachers of the "Christian Church" group, popularly designated in that generation as "New Light Christians."

Some of these worthy of mentioning are: Matthew Gardner of Adams County, Ohio. He testified: "Elder Stone usually visited Ohio once a year, and I would have matters arranged beforehand and take the tour with him."[13] Others in Ohio who travelled with Stone are: William Kinkade (See Ch. XIII), James Hughes, John Mavity, Nathan Worley, David Kirkpatrick.

In Indiana: James Robeson, Clement Nance, as mentioned.

Throughout Kentucky were numerous congregations founded by his evangelizing.

In Kentucky, naturally, Stone had developed a large following of preachers. Some of these came out of the student body of his several schools, in Lexington and Georgetown. Prominent among these were such leaders as John Rogers, brother of the veteran Samuel Rogers. John was a student of Stone's in Georgetown. (See his story in Ch. XIII.) He represented the Stone group in the joint assignment of winning the many scattered local congregations to the plan for union.

John Allen Gano was another of Stone's students at Georgetown, who expressed for him fond affection as well as profound confidence in him as a teacher and pastor. Gano became a leader of the Cause in Missouri. His son, Gen. Richard M. Gano, became a prominent leader in Texas.[14]

Indiana was greatly influenced by the Stone evangelists.

The account of the life of Elijah Goodwin reveals some of this. (See Ch. XIII.) Elijah Martindale, of Henry County, Indiana, also tells of his observations of the conflicts of opinion between the two

---

[13] Matthew Gardner, *Autobiography*, p. 33, quoted in Ware, *B.W. Stone*, p. 190.

[14] Hall, Colby D., *Texas Disciples* (Fort Worth: Texas Christian University Press, 1953), p. 356.

groups, in the period of endeavoring to complete the union.

Clement Nance, one of the three who came from Virginia to the conference at Cane Ridge in 1804 went to Indiana and became an effective evangelist. John Longley who had known Stone at Cabin Creek in the early days, wrote from Lafayette, Indiana, in 1851, words of fond remembrance of the travel with the aging elder, and the tender affection for him. The man who planted the first congregation in Indianapolis, and became outstanding as a leader of the organized missionary work of the later brotherhood, John O'Kane, had become a convert to the idea of the united church by reading Stone's *Christian Messenger*. He married the daughter of Joseph Thomas, a prominent addition from the earlier ranks of the "Christian Connection." His story is recorded in Part II.

Illinois was the home of Barton Stone himself after 1834, where he continued his periodical, the *Christian Messenger*, with the help of D. Pat Henderson, whom he had baptized in Fayette County, Kentucky, in 1832. It was at Jacksonville where he declined to take membership in either congregation until they would unite. Thus, he gave great strength to the uniting efforts.

Missouri is the state that was deeply affected by influx from Kentucky, and consequently much influenced by the disciples of Stone. Back in the pre-state days, Samuel Rogers had spent a season as a pioneer citizen, and in later years exercised his interest in the state by much evangelizing. The first evangelist of the Cause to labor in Missouri was Thomas McBride, Thomas M. Allen came from Kentucky in 1836. "The roll of Kentucky preachers in Missouri during Stone's day is impressive."[15]

Of course, Stone himself spent several months in Missouri visiting his several children who had moved there.

The extensiveness of the influence of the preachers who looked to Stone for leadership is illustrated by the case of Dr. William

---

[15] Ware, *op. cit.*, p. 292; most of the data in this section is borrowed from Ware, *op. cit.*

Defee. He was the earliest evangelist of the Movement to show up in Texas, in the year 1836, and organized the earliest congregation of "Christians." He sent in a report to Stone's paper, the *Christian Messenger.*[16]

Stone was capable of winning men of large caliber. Two examples will illustrate this. Judge Jesse M. Bledsoe (1776-1836) was known as an eminent lawyer and politician as well as a judge. Of him it was said, that "he was endowed with splendid talents, and, with the exception of Henry Clay was the most eloquent man in Kentucky."[17] He later became a Kentucky legislator, Secretary of State, and a Circuit U.S. Judge and a United States Senator. He was trained in Transylvania Seminary, and later became Professor of Common Law in that eminent institution. With such abilities and the prestige that would accompany them, he must have been a fruitful preacher.

Another man of eminence whom Stone was helpful in winning to the Cause and developing in it, was John Telemachus Johnson, of a prominent political family. His brother, Richard M. Johnson, was the ninth vice-president of the United States. Johnson was won to the Reformation idea by the writing of Alexander Campbell and tried to win the Baptist congregation at Great Crossing, Kentucky, to the new view. Since they would not follow him in this, he organized a new congregation with a membership of three, which "increased to seventy within little more than a year. This was in February, 1831."[18]

Thus, he became a neighboring pastor to Stone at Georgetown, where the latter was also conducting the Rittenhouse Academy. The two preachers recognized the similarity of their two pleas, and being of clear and pacific minds, readily agreed to make a move to get these two together. This was the real origin of the move toward

---

[16] For the story see Hall, Texas Disciples, Chap. IV, pp. 45-52.

[17] Ware, op. cit., p. 196.

[18] Ibid., p. 236.

unification of the "Reformed Baptists" of Campbell and the "Christians" of Stone, which occurred, locally in Lexington, New Year's Day, 1832, and was culminated during the next two years or more through the ministries of travel by John Smith of the "Reformers" and John Rogers of the "Christians."

If Barton Warren Stone had one all-over-prevailing quality, it was gentleness. Never did the title "gentleman" better fit any man. The following sentences are quoted somewhat at random, from John Rogers' notes on the "Character of Barton W. Stone" which he added to Stone's *Autobiography*:

> The writer of this sketch was much about the house of the venerated Stone, for many years, and it affords him peculiar pleasure to say, he never heard him speak a harsh or unkind word to any member of his family; nor does he remember to have seen him angry, during an acquaintance of a quarter of a century. ... He had learned in the school of Christ the invaluable art of self-government. . . . B.W. Stone, as a neighbor, was universally loved. On this subject, the writer speaks advisedly. If ever he had an enemy, he knows it not. The goodness of his manners, his cheerfulness, his quiet, peaceable, and obliging deportment greatly endeared him to those amongst whom he lived. . . . He possessed a gentle, meek, and quiet spirit, which, in the sight of God, is of great price. . . ."[19]

Then he tells this incident:

> A young preacher [Presbyterian] asked a person present "Of what church are you a member?"
> He replied, "Of the Christian church."
> "Do you mean the New Light church?"
> Said he, "Some call us New Lights, by way of reproach."
> "Well," said the Presbyterian preacher, "B.W. Stone has done more harm by his good conduct than by all his

---

[19] John Rogers, "Character of Barton W. Stone" in his additional chapters to Barton W. Stone's *Autobiography*, pp. 225-229.

preaching and writing: because he has lived so much like a Christian that people take him to be one."

The reply was, "Are we to judge a man's character by his good conduct or his bad?"

He replied: "A man's conduct must be good, but if he is unsound in the faith, he cannot be a Christian."

How different was Stone's scale of measurement: "A man's character is a test of Christian fellowship."[20]

Some sixty printed pages in similar strain, follow. From them we choose as an example his own counsel:

> A word to my brethren in the ministry.—My dear brethren: —Permit an old man now about to leave you, to speak plainly to you. We have a super-abundance of hard speeches against us by our sectarian neighbors, without adding to the number of them. 'Let us love one another; for love is of God.' Not long since I read an address of an Elder, to his preaching brethren. It was short, but to the very point, in these words: 'Be humble, be humble, be humble.' I adopt the language and sentiment with application to you. . . . Avoid all reproachful irritating language; it genders strife, cools brotherly love, and may, from small beginnings, end in an exterminating war.[21]

True, he engaged in some heated controversy with "orthodox" brethren, especially on such subjects as the Trinity, atonement and such. He got drawn into that without his desire or expectation. He made some comments on the theme, in personal conversation with the orthodox brother, not expecting to start an argument, least of all in print. He was astonished to find a pamphlet reply to his confidential remarks. Then he felt obliged to publish a reply, although such had never been his original intention. His one guiding principle in this abstruse and complicated field of thought throughout was to stay within the limits of scriptural expressions. In this controversial subject, Alexander Campbell at one time chided him for

---

[20] Ibid., p. 236 (a paraphrase).
[21] Ibid., p. 248.

indulging, yet in the end vindicated him and agreed that he had no taint of Arianism.

All evidence points to the conclusion: Barton W. Stone was a soul of peace, love, and gentleness. He was not built for an antagonist.

Permit the author, here to insert a personal experience that will illustrate how easily we can allow the familiarity of an experience to dull the sense of its importance in the long run of history. During the years 1899 through 1902 I was a student in the College of the Bible and Kentucky University (now Transylvania). Among my teachers were J.W. McGarvey, Charles Louis Loos, Robert Graham (retired) and I.B. Grubbs, men whose careers reached back to the period of the pioneers. They had labored in Kentucky for some years. Nevertheless, during those three years I never heard of Cane Ridge, though it was not far away. No doubt those teachers were too busy making history to take time to teach it. My first trip to Cane Ridge was many years later.

Believe me, history had mellowed by the time my students got to it.

CHAPTER X
THE "NEW LIGHTS" STRESS EMOTIONALISM AND (?) CONTINUE THE MOURNERS' BENCH

The current disciples of the "Nineteenth-Century Reformation" may be surprised—even shocked—to learn that their forbears in the faith practiced what we now call the "mourners' bench" technique. That they did so, and even often called it by that name, is obvious to the readers of these biographies of "New Light" preachers, as they appear in these pages. For example, Samuel Rogers: "We had mourners' benches in those days."[1] What a contrast these, with the sober preaching and logical arguments of the evangelists of the later days!

But those who are surprised need not let it go any farther—may save the shock! For, as in so many instances in the study of history, a little scrap of history needs to be explained by a little more history, the background. We need to take into consideration the previous period, and what conditions and assumptions it bequeathed to its successor.

Hence, we undertake in the next paragraph or so, to refresh the minds of our readers with the contents of our Chapter II with its story of the rise and development of Christian evangelism in young America. That is a long and complicated history, so full of lines of influence that we hesitated to try to cover it in one chapter, lest the readers bog down in too long a story. Now we shall undertake to express the basic principles of that long story in capsule form, hoping to clarify the philosophy of it. This may be found in the following five propositions:

(1) The new American sense of personal "liberty," hence responsibility, together with the release from the reliance of the State

---

[1] 1. Samuel Rogers, Autobiography, p. 44.

Church for responsibility for his religion, led the American citizen to claim and to recognize that his religion was up to him, personally.

(2) This personal freedom, together with the continuous struggles with wars and primitive conditions, led to a very much lower general level of moral standards (only about 10 percent of the people acknowledged membership in or obligation to any church.)

(3) The dominant theology was Calvinism, which required for conversion, a mystical experience, interpreted as being a divine visitation of "regeneration," toward which the sinner had no power of his own to move; being dependent wholly on the initiation of the Holy Spirit. This left him impotent and helpless.

(4) The effort to help the seekers to achieve this mystical "experience" induced the evangelistically inclined preachers to appeal strongly to the emotions of their hearers, developing a custom known as the "mourners' bench," of emotional excitability. (Preachers of Old Side opposed revivals; New Side developed them.)

(5) In the western migrations this emotionalism was met and enhanced by frontier conditions of loneliness, the breaking off from old home ties, lack of schooling and reading, and a sense of individualism; so that the camp-meeting developed a type of emotional preaching and excitability of climactic intensity. (Cane Ridge 1801, for example.)

The extreme effort of one Bible-loving preacher (Barton W. Stone) to achieve this prescribed emotional experience, led him to discover the New Testament teaching that "faith comes by hearing . . . the Word of God," through the use of the ordinary rational processes of the mind. This released the requirement of excessive emotionalism and ushered in the period of "Reformation of the Nineteenth Century."

We would not want to be regarded as calling in question, denying, or doubting the sincerity of the many good people who still believe in this theory of "experimental religion," here identified as

Calvinism.[2] Hence we quote next from one of the most distinguished psychologists of America, his explanation of the psychology of the emotional experience. He is Professor William James (1841-1910) of Harvard University. He shows how this cataclysmic psychology, used in conversion, comes about so easily, and even naturally, to many people; and how it can be explained normally on psychological principles:

> In the fully evolved Revivalism of Great Britain and America, we have, so to speak, a codified and stereotyped procedure, to which this way of thinking led. In spite of the unquestionable fact that saints of the once-born type exist, that there may be a gradual growth in holiness without the cataclysm; in spite of the slow leakage (as one may say) of much mere natural goodness into the scheme of salvation; revivalism has always assumed that only its own type of religious experience can be perfect; you must first be nailed to the cross of natural despair and agony, and then, in the twinkling of an eye be miraculously released.
>
> It is natural that those who personally traverse such an experience should carry away a feeling of its being a miracle rather than a natural process. Voices are often heard, lights seen, or visions witnessed; automatic phenomena occur, and it always seems, after the surrender of the personal will, as if an extraneous higher will had flooded in and taken possession. Moreover, the sense of renovation, safety, cleanness, rightness, can be marvelous, and jubilant, as well to warrant one's belief in a radically new substantial nature.[3]

Thus, expressed in the careful and calculated terms of the philosopher, we can readily trace the experience of many of whom we have read, perhaps heard. But it would have to be heated up by the emotional passion of the moment of experience. Go back to Chap-

---

[2] We are quite aware that "Calvinism" covers much more than this theory of "Experimental Religion." It is used here in the popular sense.

[3] William James, The Varieties of Religious Experience, (Modern Library Edition, New York: Random House, 1929.) pp. 223-224.

ter III and re-read the experience of Barton W. Stone. There you may be able to trace the psychological pattern, described by Professor James. Note especially that first experience, after he heard the sermon on "God is love," and seriously assumed that he had had the required emotional experience—until he had the insight, later, into the new concept of intelligent faith, founded on evidence.

After that "experience," he knew that faith is based on testimony and "these are written that ye may believe, and believing, have life through his name"; that the seeker does his own deciding, with his own powers. True, emotions arise in the heart, even then. But it was the effect, rather than the cause of the faith. And the rational man was involved; not just the emotional alone.

This condensed review of the background has made clear, we hope, that the earliest basic principle of this new reformation was the principle of a rational faith based on Biblical testimony, achieved by normal human rational processes of the mind, involving, as an effect, only the normal amount of emotionalism, varying according to the disposition of the several individuals.

Let us pause here to remind ourselves that this very same principle was brought out by the Campbells, years later (1811-12 and 1827) and powerful use was made of it, especially in the evangelistic preaching of Walter Scott. Alexander Campbell, in applying this doctrine, bore down on his opposition to the use of "feelings" as an evidence of conversion, so strenuously that he is generally credited as the modern discoverer of the doctrine of "faith based on testimony." We have observed herein that Stone encountered this truth as early as 1800, and used it in his evangelism, and enlisted his fellow-evangelists in the teaching of it from that time forward. That was a dozen years before Campbell encountered the doctrine, and twenty-seven years before it was put to use in evangelism.

But there was one notable difference between these two devoted preachers in the utilization of the new doctrine: Campbell and Scott made a clean break with emotionalism. They argued against any emotional experience as evidence of pardon, and discouraged all expression of emotional feelings in the process of conversion.

Stone met the situation differently. He continued the use of emotional expression, prayers for the seeker and rejoicing over conversion.

And that is the point of this chapter. Historically and psychologically, why did Stone continue the practice which was ruled out by the logic of his new doctrine, which he himself said had been "received" by him (in about 1800) ?[4]

Having gone through the story of the rise of revivals in young America, and having observed the development of high emotionalism as a part of the process, and how it fitted into the psychology and social conditions of the frontier, we can well understand how Stone followed a different route from that of the Campbells.

Stone had grown up on the frontier. He had gone through the heat and fire of the revivals. The most famous one of them all, "Cane Ridge," summer, 1801, was in the church of which he was the pastor. It was from about that date that his new reform began. The people of the frontier were his people. Several of the preachers of his group have testified that they had grown up to manhood, knowing no other way of "getting religion."

This was the generation of Stone. These were his people. He spoke and lived their language. These were the folkways of his generation. If they were to listen to him, he must speak the language they both knew.

How different was the background of the Campbells! They came up through the unexpressive, unemotional, Scotch old-school Calvinism. They probably never heard any shouting at a religious gathering in their early days. Both of them, father and son, assumed that they had gone through the expected "experience" in orthodox fashion although we are sure that it was more intellectual

---

[4] "As might be expected, many objections arose in my mind against the doctrine just received by me" Stone, *Autobiography*, p. 34.

than emotional.

Alexander Campbell was not an evangelistic preacher as Richardson clearly points out.[5] He was a debater, concerned in getting the doctrine clarified, not in converting sinners. There were no great "meetings" of evangelistic nature among them until the work of Walter Scott in 1827.

Both Campbell and Stone were strongly intellectual; but Stone was natively emotional and Campbell almost exclusively intellectual. But the chief difference lay in their differing backgrounds.

Singing was one of the chief expressions of the emotionalism of public worship as always. Mr. Campbell was interested in this. He was the publisher of songbooks. The "Christians" had a Hymnal long before the "Reformers." Rice Haggard published a Hymnal "for the brotherhood" sometime about 1818.[6] We have no existing copies of his book, however, so our historians are excusable for having overlooked it.[7] Campbell was a publisher, and a good business man; Stone could not claim that talent; and Haggard died too soon to look after the circulation of his Hymnal.

Customary thinking becomes imbedded in our hymns and songs. And singing played a large part in revivalism. The camp-meeting songs that preceded the "New Light" period did not fit the new concept of conversion; they all assumed the old cataclysmic pattern. To be sure, an understanding person could read into the old songs the newer significance. Personally, I did this very thing, in the old enthusiastic Christian Endeavor days of the early 1900's, along with my Cumberland Presbyterian and Methodist friends. For example:

---

[5] Richardson, Memoirs of A. Campbell, II, 199.

[6] Cobb, ed., *Forgotten Soldier*, pp. 61, 64, including a quote from J. P. Barrett (The Centennial of Religious Journalism), who dates the Hymnal 1818.

[7] For instance, C.C. Ware (*B.W. Stone*) says, "Perhaps the first Christian hymn book of the brotherhood was that of Stone and Johnson published in Georgetown before 1832." (p. 287.) [NOTE: Since the time this volume was written, a copy of the book has been found, and is available to view on Archive.org.—*Editor.*]

"At the cross, at the cross,
where I first saw the light
And the burden of my heart rolled away,
'Twas there by faith,
I received my sight,
And now I am happy all the day."

The composer of that song, and almost everybody who sang it, doubtless saw in that old camp-meeting song the standard mourners' bench experience. When I sang it, I thought of my calm confession of faith, based on evidence, and sang on. The "New Lights" and Brother Stone might have done the same thing, as they continued to sing the same old songs and sing into them the newer, richer significance. For he was a patient teacher.

We can better understand and appreciate his patience and his delay if we go back and recall the episode of his attempt to preach the doctrine of "baptism for the remission of sins." You recall that it was so new and so different that it confused the people. It fell flat; he deferred it until "it was revived by Alexander Campbell some years after."[8]

Under this revised conception of faith, let us inquire "What room is left for the emotions?" Certainly no one expects emotions to be eliminated, entirely. Some opponents of Alexander Campbell accused him of doing this very thing, and some of his followers almost did so. But never Barton W. Stone!! And never any thoughtful student of the New Testament; and certainly, not any historian of the period of the "New Light" Christians. For what sincere Christian disciple can ever forget his own warmth of heart, joy of soul, and enthusiasm of the entire being, that accompanied his confession of faith in Christ as Lord, and his burial by baptism to express this dedication of life to Him! These are the normal "feelings" on such an occasion; the results of the action taken.

From the heading of this chapter we might ask: "Why did the

---

[8] Stone, *Autobiography*, p. 56-57.

"New Lights" stress emotionalism and (?) continue the Mourners' Bench?" It is thus awkwardly divided because they did not actually continue the "mourners' bench" technique. For they had eliminated the key doctrine of "Calvinism" that made the mourners' bench experience what it was, and had been, through many years of revivals: a stumbling-block in the way of seekers after salvation. This was the discovery of Barton W. Stone, in his "experience" of 1800. After he "received the doctrine," the "New Lights" preached differently: faith based on testimony of the Holy Spirit through the Bible. They continued the emotional expressions beyond our expectation, to be sure. It was the language of the generation, as has been pointed out. They had learned it as they learned their songs. But it was not genuinely the "mourners' bench," although it was confusing.

Having cleared the theory, let us inquire, now, What element of feeling could Stone have sensed in all this emotionalism under the new conception of faith? It must have been a genuine, sincere emotional expression, or Stone would not have encouraged it.

In doing this, let us not stand off a century and more later and envision it from the long distance of our own generation with our modern notions of preaching, singing and such. Let us, as best we may, stand by the side of the gentle, genuine Stone, and see the events, as best we can, as he saw them then.

We must remember that Stone was not only an evangelist; he was also a school teacher; as such he knew full well that the acceptance of a new view-point requires time—and patience. By experience, he learned patience and caution. He was not the only teacher who needed patience in introducing a new conception. It was fifteen years, after Alexander Campbell first conceived the doctrine of faith based on testimony (1812) before it was preached actively in evangelism by Walter Scott, in 1827. And then he presented the new doctrine with caution and trepidation. He even went outside the bounds of the Mahoning Association (his employers at the time) to present it, lest the brethren should criticize him for teaching something new and different. And, notably, the teaching of it, on that occasion, fell flat. It did not go over until at a later meeting at New Lisbon, when Mr. Amends, a unique case, accepted the doctrine, having heard only the last paragraph or so of the sermon. That fortunate incident made it succeed.[9] But that was after fifteen years of patient waiting. Stone had to wait longer than that. He had no providential Mr. Amends!

We may be reminded that other reformers had similar experiences to press patience into their processes, such as Luther and Calvin.[10]

To Barton W. Stone, also, the "Gift of the Holy Spirit" was not a mere verbal expression, as it seems to be to many modern disciples of Jesus. As he judged the validity of the "bodily exercises" at the Logan County revival in 1801 by the fact that lives were changed for the good, so the Spirit was a reality to him. Perhaps he was patient with those seekers at the "altar," in hope that they would acquire the "gifts of the Spirit." For he believed in these gifts as a matter of everyday religion. All records testify that Stone lived these "gifts of the Spirit"; "love, joy, peace, patience, kindness, goodness, faithfulness, gentleness, self-control; against such there is no law" (Gal. 5:22). He was anxious for his disciples to cultivate or achieve them. Doubtless his praying with the penitents at the "altar" had in mind the development of these "fruits of the Spirit." So long as he could nourish such a hope, he would be slow to discourage the practice which he described, as "mourners were invited every day to collect before the stand, in order for prayers (this being the custom of the time)."[11]

Can we visualize such an atmosphere; emotionalism without the crying, groaning, beseeching, confessing; wailing for sins, then

---

[9] Richardson, *Memoirs*, II, 209-212.

[10] Luther postponed teaching adult immersion, lest the people conclude he was teaching them a new baptism. Calvin wanted to observe the communion every Sunday, but the people overruled him, by declining.

[11] Stone, *Autobiography*, p. 56.

at the same time, rejoicing? Those of us who lived through the period of evangelism at about the turn of the twentieth century may well duplicate the scene, in the days between, say J.V. Updike, and Charles Reign Scoville (about 1890 to 1930). The joyous singing, the thrill at the invitation song, the personal workers going from one prospect to another—all produced a feeling of emotion that was genuine, effective, and without a touch of the old mourners' bench psychology.

Personally, I can testify. Through those days of what has sometimes been called "professional evangelists," came my growing up. In a revival by J.V. Updike, in McPherson, Kansas, in (about) 1888, I recall, vividly the coming of my dear elderly "Aunt Bettie" to my side, during the long and exciting invitation hymn, urging me to go forward. Emotion? The whole tabernacle thrilled with it. I proved myself able to resist it, partly, I now judge, because I had been indoctrinated in that direction. Later, at sixteen, I made my confession and was buried in baptism; with much emotion (controlled, nevertheless), keen and deep emotion. Yes, there can be emotion, with the mourners' bench or "Calvinism"!

There was some definite, beneficent effect coming to the seekers after religion, which Stone held in his philosophy of the matter and which he observed as lacking in the thought of the Campbells. This missing element was mentioned by Stone in his account of the first meetings of the two leaders in 1824:

> I thought then that he [Campbell] was not sufficiently explicit on the influence of the Spirit, which led many honest Christians to think he denied them.[12]

Obviously Campbell must have improved along this line, later, for Stone continues: "Had he been as explicit then, as since, many honest souls would have been still with us, and would have greatly aided the good cause." Whether this margin of difference was some physical expression akin to shouting, or the evidences of the

---

[12] Ibid., p. 70.

presence of the "fruits of the Spirit," we know not. There is little if any doubt that the legalistic spirit of some of Campbell's disciples in placing all emphasis on immersion made the neglect of the Spirit quite obvious. For it is certain that this literalist attitude was unwisely held by many of them.

We are fortunate in having the *Autobiography of Samuel Rogers*, a Timothy of Barton W. Stone, and a "man of the people," with limited schooling and the typical frontier feeling. In one passage in his self-story he reveals something of his love of fellowship.

> After a brief discourse [by Rogers] or rather exhortation, we sang and prayed, and sang again and again, the congregation mingling and commingling in the old-fashioned exercise of shaking hands, which I wish we could have restored now, instead of so much stiffness and formality, as we have in our worship. The sermon now is the great event of the day's worship, and little else is talked about or thought of as the attraction to the house of the Lord. The disciples anciently met together to break bread, and the chief entertainment, from all we can gather, was the reading and expounding of the Scriptures, singing psalms, and hymns, and spiritual songs, and making melody in their hearts. ... [13]

That was not all that Brother Rogers wished to have perpetuated. He also wrote:

> We had mourners' benches in those days, and they were things unauthorized by the Word of God. We long since abolished them, and we did right in so doing; but I almost fear that we did it in such a way as to abolish the mourners too. [14]

Was this mere nostalgia? His expressions impress me that it

---

[13] Samuel Rogers, *Autobiography*, p. 29. One of the experiences etched distinctly in my childish memory (about six), is of a meeting of this sort. I wondered, "Why the tears in their eyes?"

[14] Ibid., p. 44.

was much more than nostalgia. He felt something solid in the customs, which, seemingly, had been laid aside.

Moreover, the yearning for more emotional expression did not disappear promptly. There are records of well-settled preachers longing for the older customs. And this sentiment came from some whose lives did not reach back as far as the emotional period. Here is one example from Brother B.F. Manire, who was preaching as late as 1900. In his "Reminiscences of Preachers in Mississippi," Manire expresses himself thus:

> Joshua K. Speer was not the most learned, nor logical nor eloquent, but he was by far, the most emotional preacher I have ever known. He not only felt, himself, but he made others feel. He not only wept, himself, but he made others weep. I can see him now as the tears rolled down his cheeks, while he talked of Jesus and his love. Old as I am now, and short as time now left for me to serve my Master, I would give all the wealth of a Gould or a Vanderbilt, if I had it, for the power, the gift of exhortation which he possessed.
>
> Most of our pioneer preachers were good exhorters, and to that fact their success in a great measure was due. Since that day our preachers have developed a logical ability that is truly wonderful, but have lost, it seems to me, almost unanimously, the power to move the hearts of men. ... We have debaters enough, in fact enough on hand to last a generation.[15]

Many a preacher today may well sympathize with Brother Manire's lament for more emotional preaching, especially those who have to subsist on the legalistic preaching of the debater type, must certainly sympathize with Brother Manire's longing.

The striking aspect of this testimony is that Mr. Manire was of the intellectual type rather than emotional. He was well educated, cultured, and refined. I can understand his longing for more emo-

---

[15] This "Reminiscence" is contained in M.F. Harmon: *A History of the Christian Church in Mississippi* (Aberdeen, Miss., 1929).

tionalism, for myself. And that fact makes his testimony the more valuable in his estimate of the value of some share of emotionalism in the preaching brethren.

From a period much farther back than Manire's comes a surprising testimony which seems to point in the same direction, the words of even Walter Scott. The beloved W.A. Fortune in his *Disciples in Kentucky* writes,

> Walter Scott, in a letter written on August 4, 1840, which is in the P.S. Fall Collection, refers to a statement concerning the sectarianism of the Disciples, which Mr. Fall had made in a recent letter, he said, "When you express your doubts of the matters connected with the recent Reformation, I sympathize with you, for the thing has not been what I hoped it would be by a thousand miles. We are indeed a 'sect' differing but little, of anything that is good, from many of the parties around us. Alas, my soul is grieved every day." (page 170)

Can it be that this extraordinary evangelist among the early preachers felt that the ordinary evangelist had turned his "five finger exercise" into a device entirely too legalistic, now that he longed for more of the spirit in the process of conversion? Let us hope so. If he did he will be joined by many of his modern followers.

It was providential that the streams of Stone and Campbell flowed together. Our present task demands the strength of both of them. Perhaps Barton W. Stone had a discerning spirit. He made the acquaintance with the Holy Spirit, beyond his fellows of his own period, or of ours.

After I had written the above chapter, I learned that my old-time college-mate in the College of the Bible (1901-02), John B. Hunley, of Virginia, had just published his autobiography under the title *A Spiritual Argosy*. Knowing of his special interest in devotional thinking and his firm faith in the leadings of the Holy Spirit, I read the book with eager expectation. Nor was I disappointed. Frankly and frequently, he chides his preaching brethren among the Disciples. Here is a sample:

> Alas, we did not speak where the Bible speaks except in part. We were strong on first principles for which we could readily give book, chapter, and verse, and rightly so, but we avoided whole sections of the Bible on such themes as Christian stewardship, Scriptural holiness—the sanctification without which no man shall see the Lord (Heb. 12:14), the new Testament emphasis on the Holy Spirit, which featured the writings of Dr. Richardson and others, and which, because of the extreme emotionalism of a century ago and later we almost wholly ignored. ... I do not see that because others had ignored or abused these truths, I should pass them by.[16]

This is just a sample of his repeated appeals for a fuller recognition and use of the privileges and power of the Holy Spirit, in many ways.

---

[16] John B. Nunley, *A Spiritual Argosy*, Christopher, 1958.

CHAPTER XI
THE "NEW LIGHTS" DISSOLVE, AND "SINK INTO UNION" WITH THE BODY OF CHRISTIAN-DISCIPLES

This is the story of the "New Light" Christians.

They had been alive, active and somewhat steadily growing for nearly twenty years before they heard of the Campbell movement. The latter had been a disturbance within the Presbyterian fold in western Pennsylvania, beginning in 1809, then, after adopting immersion in 1812, within the Baptist. Alexander Campbell's first debate, that with Walker in 1820, drew only local notoriety, but his coming to Kentucky in 1823 to debate with McCalla, "created great excitement," according to Stone's report. Also, it aroused, within the Christian group, the recognition of a kindred movement.

The first impressions of the leaders of these two groups, each on the other, were remarkably favorable. Mr. Campbell had occasion to express his impression of Stone in the *Christian Baptist* in 1828, as follows:

> Your enemies, and they are not a few, have, to a man, as far as I have heard them speak, said your Christian character, your moral deportment, was unblemished. Would to Heaven that this could be said of all who opposed you.
>
> I do not think it strange that, in running posthaste out of Babylon, you should have, in some angles of your course, run past Jerusalem. Nay, verily, I have been astonished that you should have made so few aberrations in so many efforts.
>
> But Brother Stone, I exceedingly regret that you have said and written on two topics, which neither you nor myself nor any man living can fully understand.
>
> Wishing you favor, mercy and peace, from God our Father and the Lord Jesus Christ, and that you may never set

up a new sect, I'm yours in the Lord. Editor.[1]

Stone's expression about Campbell came, after years of ripening, in his Autobiography. It is so genuine that it must be what he felt during his more active years. It reads:

> Till the period when Alexander Campbell, of Virginia, appeared and caused a great excitement on the subject of religion in Kentucky and other states "Some said he is a good man, but others said, 'Nay but he deceiveth the people.'" When he came into Kentucky I heard him often in public and in private. I was pleased with his manner and matter. I saw no distinctive features between the doctrine he preached and that which we had preached for many years except on the subject of baptism for the remission of sins. Even this I had once received and taught, as before stated, but strangely let it go from my mind, till Brother Campbell revived it afresh.[2]

Then he becomes more specific, as he thinks through the years of experience that had passed, and adds:

> I thought that he was not sufficiently explicit on the influence of the Spirit, which led many honest Christians to think he denied them. Had he been as explicit then, as since, many honest souls would have been still with us, and would have greatly aided the good cause. In a few things I dissented from him, but was agreed to disagree.[3]

Next, he adds a summary conclusion, which was worth the whole of what he had said before. They were golden words for the future outlook.

> I will not say, there are no faults in Brother Campbell: but that there are fewer, perhaps, in him than any man I know on earth; and over those few my love would throw a

---

[1] *The Christian Baptist*, as revised by David S. Burnett, 2d edition, 7 vols. in one; Vol. V, p. 380.

[2] 2. Stone, *Autobiography*, p. 70.

[3] Ibid.

veil and hide them from view forever. I am constrained, and willingly constrained to acknowledge him as the greatest promoter of this reformation of any man living. The Lord reward him.[4]

But with all of his high regard for Brother Campbell, he was not to be awed by his eminence nor challenged by his theology. Promptly, frankly (if not modestly in Campbell's opinion), he recognized this relationship he bore to the doughty Baptist Reformer—that of his predecessor in reform. And he proceeded to list the points in which he had been there before the "Reformed Baptists."[5]

1. For thirty years the Christians have taught that Sectarianism is anti-Christian. The Reformers "teach the same."
2. For thirty years the Christians have taught that all Christians should unite in one body. The Reformers "teach the same."
3. For thirty years Christians have taught that authoritative creeds and confessions are "strong props" of sectarianism and should be abandoned. The Reformers "teach the same."
4. For thirty years the Christians have preached the gospel to every creature on the basis that its own testimony can produce faith and obedience in the rational creature. The Reformers "teach the same."
5. For thirty years the Christians have taught that through faith "the Holy Spirit of promise," and every other promise of the New Testament is given to the renewed sinner. The Reformers "teach the same."
6. Years ago, many of the Christians preached baptism, as a means, in connection with faith and repentance, for the remission of sins, and the gift of the Holy Spirit. The Reformers "preach the same" and "extended it farther" than the Christians.

---

[4] Ibid.

[5] From the *Christian Messenger*, Vol. V (1831), p. 180, quoted from West., *op. cit.*, p. 142.

   7. For thirty years the Christians have rejected all names, but Christians. The Reformers acknowledge this name as proper, but seem to prefer another.[6]

This list of points held in common was surely very impressive. But, obviously, it impressed Mr. Campbell at the wrong points of emphasis. Evidently, the redundant repetition of phrases and the several quotation marks were intended to emphasize the large amount of agreements, but Campbell received them rather as "a squinting of some sort of precedence of priority in the claims" of the Christians, in having discovered the principles of the "Reformation," before his own followers had appeared on the American scene.[7] Hence, as West says, "Campbell betrayed little enthusiasm for the merger." What he evidently perceived was too much fact in the intimation of the priority of the plea by the Christians. For final history has turned these intimations of Stone into actual, provable history. During the later years, comment on this priority of the "Christians" has been passed over for the most part, without comment; it was not an active issue. And it need not be now; and is not now, except for history. The first writer to exercise the boldness to express the idea, seemingly, was Professor E.E. Snoddy, of the College of the Bible. In his Introduction to C.C. Ware's *Barton Warren Stone*, in 1932, he wrote:

> Historians of the Disciples of Christ have never felt any necessity of taking Barton W. Stone and his ideals into account in their efforts to reconstruct historically the origin of the Disciples of Christ.
>
> This conception of Stone and his movement is wholly unwarranted by historical fact. To Stone belongs priority in time, priority in American experience, priority in the ideal of unity, priority in evangelism, priority in the independen-

---

   [6] We may pause to observe that Stones' choice of "thirty years" would indicate that those new teachings began as early as 1800. And Stone was not loose with his figures. That date corresponds with the calculations in this text.

   [7] Campbell's own words. See West, *op. cit.*, p. 143.

cy of his movement, priority in the complete renunciation of the Calvinistic system of theology, and finally, priority in sacrificial devotion to his cause.[8]

It could be an invitation and a challenge to a serious-minded student of the history of the Movement, to test out each of these "priorities" by the details of the history as related in this volume. The author confesses that Professor Snoddy's words have lent encouragement to him as he followed out this theme. Indeed, he is conscious of having added to the list of "priorities."

There were several other "spats" back and forth between the two leaders, of much the same flavor, but as Stone expressed it, they "agreed to disagree."[7] As will be observed later, throughout the process of unifying, Campbell was more neutral rather than enthusiastic.

The final fusion of the two groups, as the historian views it, was practically inevitable. Their aims were virtually identical, their principles much the same, and their leadership, although pleased with fixed concepts and sufficient stubbornness, nevertheless were endowed with a sufficiency of the Spirit of their Master to respect each other and yield for the advantage of common Cause to which they were genuinely devoted.

The spark of leadership for this unification also appeared in Kentucky. The Spirit of God obviously moved in the hearts of two of His servants in the community of Georgetown, Kentucky. The one was John T. Johnson, who had been won to the views of Alexander Campbell by reading the *Christian Baptist*, and had withdrawn from the local Great Crossings Baptist Church, when he could not induce them to follow him, and was presently ministering to a group of Reformed Baptists, recognized as of the Campbell following. The other was Barton W. Stone himself, currently head of a private school in Georgetown and also minister of the Christian "New Light" church there. Both of these preachers were

---

[8] Professor E. E. Snoddy in Introduction to C.C. Ware, *B.W. Stone*, p. xi.

men of high caliber, respectful of each other, and devoid of selfish ambition and aims for personal notoriety. They were persuaded that the two movements were sufficiently alike to become one, and that the Cause of Christian union would be greatly strengthened by such a merger. They plainly saw that some action was needed to get them started, so they determined to initiate the process—at home. They not only prayed to the Lord, "Please let us unite"; they added, "beginning with us."

So, they called a conference of both of their peoples in Georgetown for four days preceding Christmas, 1831. This was succeeded by a similar one in Lexington, for the four days preceding and culminating on New Year's Day, 1832. John Smith ("Raccoon") and Stone were the leading speakers. The spark struck fire; the union of these local forces was affected. Realizing that their principle of local congregational independence required local action, they proceeded with wisdom, as well as caution. They commissioned two brethren to travel among the churches to teach the concept of the union and to secure local official action for unification of the local congregations. The two preachers were John Smith, of the Campbell group, and John Rogers of the Christians. This process was slow and often tedious, but it was wise. More than two years were required to contact all the congregations.

There were hitches, here and there, which caused delay. One famous case was that of Jacksonville, Illinois, where Barton Stone had moved his residence. He notified the two separate congregations that he would join neither of them until they joined each other.[9] This effected the union, and set an impressive example. The union action prevailed generally throughout Kentucky, much in Ohio and other states. Efforts to induce the "Christian Connection" brethren to join in the move were unsuccessful. Stone labored hard to win the Eastern Christians, although Campbell was not favorable to this. He objected because they were tainted too strongly with

---

[9] Stone, *Autobiography*, p. 73.

the belief in Unitarianism.[10]

Mr. Campbell did nothing to oppose or delay the process; he also did little to speed it forward. The process was going forward, outside his immediate territory; he stood aside and let it pass. As early as 1828 he had published in his *Christian Baptist*, in reply to the inquiry of a subscriber

> If there is a difference between us, we know it not. We have nothing in us to prevent a union; if they have nothing in them in opposition to it, we are in spirit one. May God strengthen the cords of Christian union.[11]

The detailed story of the process of unification has been well told by the several historians of the period. These which we present here may help to make more clear the portion which the Christian group contributed, hence make the characteristics and contributions more readily discerned.[12]

The question of the relative numbers contributed to the union by each group is not discussed much in the records and histories available. Doubtless no scholar has invested in the study of Barton W. Stone more meticulous attention to details of locations and accuracy of figures than C.C. Ware. So his conclusion is worth accepting:

> They [Christians] had grown steadily. Their fellowship numbered some eight thousand. The Reformers, led by the

---

[10] West, in his *Barton W. Stone*, affords a more complete study of this phase, in his Chapter XII.

[11] Quoted from Garrison and DeGroot, *op. cit.*, p. 208.

[12] West in his *Barton Warren Stone* has three chapters on the unification process, VII, IX and X. Also one chapter of especial value on Stone's attempt to enlist the Eastern Christians. Ware's story on the unification is told in Chap. XVII, with some important aftermath in the next two. Garrison and DeGroot's condensation, including some reports on numbers, is found in Chap. V. Garrison and DeGroot, while giving less space to this period than others, relate some aspects not mentioned by others. The same may be said of Garrison's *Religion Follows the Frontier* (New York: Harper & Bros., 1931).

Campbells and Walter Scott, had about an equal number. They had been in Kentucky since 1823. Their growth had been phenomenal.[13]

The Reformers had turned so many Baptists to their way that they probably caught up with the Christians, although, at the first of their awareness of kinship, the Christians were more numerous, both in members and in congregations. Of course, statistics in that period were not available.

We have an incidental remark on the subject by one who has the qualifications of being a competent observer. For John Rogers, along with "Raccoon" John Smith, spent more than two years in "riding" among the churches of these two groups, to persuade them into an active unity. He must have had the information at hand. In combatting the remarks of an opponent of both sides, a Mr. John L. Waller, in the *Western Baptist Review* (Vol. 1 number 4), wrote a satirical article against B.W. Stone, as the one who "stirred" the "New Light Stir." In his effort to deride Stone, he remarked concerning the numerical progress:

> He formed quite a respectable party. . . . But his career seemed to be run and his party on the wane, when it was taken under the supervision of Mr. Campbell, and the reformation in Kentucky, and in the west (in many instances, the most valuable part of it) is composed of the materials gathered by Mr. Stone.[14]

Rogers recognized Waller as a witness prejudiced against both groups and the entire idea of the reformation, and then he himself testified as a competent witness:

> In my judgment (and I think I ought to know as much about this matter as any man in Kentucky) we were never enjoying as great or greater prosperity, than about that period. I think I am within the bounds of truth, when I say, that

---

[13] Ware, *B.W. Stone*, p. 239.

[14] Stone, *Autobiography*, p. 343.

about the time of the Union, the people called Christians, associated with B.W. Stone numbered about eight to ten thousand, in Kentucky. We were not on the wane then but greatly on the increase.[15]

Surely after his travels for more than two years among the churches in Kentucky, Rogers must be admitted as a reliable witness on the state of progress and on the numbers. We are not assured by the figures quoted in Garrison and DeGroot (p. 115), because of the apparent or possible confusion with the Christian Connection.[16] In any event, we may look back over the period of evangelism of both groups (Scott's began in 1827); Stone's had been thriving since 1807, at least; and safely conclude that the "Christians" had much the more numerous followers. More grateful can we be that the distinction between the two groups so rapidly and successfully disappeared.

In the light of the discussion in our present volume, we deem it fitting to call attention to the difference between these leaders, as brought out by Campbell's biographer, Dr. Robert Richardson, in his official *Memoirs*. He introduces the theme:

> While the features of this organization [i.e. Stone's group] were thus, in good measure similar to those of the Reformation in which Mr. Campbell was engaged, there were some characteristic differences. With the former [Stone], the idea of uniting all men under Christ was predominant; with the latter, the desire of an exact conformity

---

[15] Ibid., p. 346.

[16] The figures there quoted are from the *Morning Star and City Watchman*, published by Elias Smith, which reprints from the *Christian Register* a report on the membership of the "Christian Connexion in the West" by states: Kentucky 3,350; Tennessee 1,800; Alabama 600; Ohio 4,390; Indiana 1,200; Illinois 600; Missouri 1,000; total 12,940. (NOTE: Elias Smith and company viewed Barton W. Stone as one of their brethren, and considered the congregations with which he was associated as faithful brethren—until around the time Stone joined forces with the "Reformers" associated with Campbell. Then the "Christian Connection" distanced themselves from Stone.—*Editor*.)

to the primitive faith and practice. The one occupied itself chiefly in casting abroad the sweeping net of the gospel, which gathers fish of every kind; the other was more intent upon collecting "the good into vessels" and casting "the bad away." Hence the former engaged mainly in preaching—the latter in teaching.[17]

Dr. Richardson has surely expressed the case with exactness, as we have followed the story herein. His further picturization of the case seems somewhat surprising, although just as exact:

> There had indeed been almost an entire neglect of evangelism on the part of the few churches which were originally connected with Mr. Campbell and his reformatory efforts. They had not a single itinerant preacher, and, although they made great progress in Biblical knowledge, they gained comparatively few converts.[18] [Observe that Richardson is referring to the period prior to 1824.]

It has been generally recognized that Walter Scott was the flame of zeal who touched off the doctrines of Campbell into evangelism. And when the younger man did this very thing with such prominent results, both of the Campbells were surprised— even shocked. The elder, Thomas Campbell, has recorded his case of shock, in his own measured, dignified phraseology, thus:

> We have long known the theory, and have spoken and published many things correctly concerning the ancient gospel, its simplicity and perfect adaptation to the present state of mankind for the benign and precious purposes of his immediate relief and complete salvation; but I must confess that in respect to the direct exhibition and application of it for that blessed purpose, I am present for the first time upon the ground where the thing has appeared to be practically exhibited to the proper purpose.[19]

---

[17] Richardson, *Memoirs*, II, 198-199.

[18] Ibid., p. 199

[19] Quoted in Garrison and DeGroot, *op. cit.* p. 189.

Indeed, Dr. Richardson, having the good advantage of close personal contact with the original actors in this drama, has recorded, in detail, the very conversations of the several active evangelists at the time.[20] This passage includes an account of Scott's first effort to present the doctrine of "baptism for the remission of sins," and its failure. It is striking that this same attempt and the same failure occurred in the cases of Stone more than a dozen years previously.

Several interesting facts come to light from this conversation recorded by Richardson here, in addition to the similar experiences of Scott and Stone. One is that it was Scott—not Campbell—who worked this doctrine into practical preaching use. The other is that doubtless Stone never knew this latter fact, for he had gone home before Richardson wrote his book.

Thus, under Providential guidance, in ways that humans would perhaps not have devised, the fusion of these two kindred forces was accomplished. As planned in the June 28, 1804, meeting at Cane Ridge, they "dissolved and sank into union with" the Christian-Disciples brotherhood—the nearest thing available to the "Body of Christ at large."

---

[20] Ibid., pp. 205-210. See also chapter VIII of this book.

CHAPTER XII
THE TOWERING FIGURE
OF ALEXANDER CAMPBELL

The design of this volume has been to bring to the fore, the story of the "New Light" Christian group. At no time has there been any purpose of displacing any other person. Particularly is there no desire to diminish the figure of any leader among the "Reformers," especially Alexander Campbell. History has a way of taking care of such matters, without the consent of any. This chapter is written largely to show that all of the claims made for this modest group herein are consistent with the career and personality of both Alexander Campbell and Barton W. Stone.

No human could have devised the story of the "Reformation of the Nineteenth Century." It grew up. We believe that Providence had a hand in it. But the story is ours to study. One thing is clear: Two strong personalities were provided for the leadership. And in the end, one of them held a pre-eminence, as the leader. Let us examine and ascertain who and why.

We have quoted Richardson's analysis of differences between Stone and Campbell, but that was only in part. Stone's outstanding features of character have been suggested in the closing paragraph of the chapter (VII) that climaxed his story. His most obvious virtue was gentleness. He was not a fighter. He never held a debate, in that generation of debating. He had plenty of opportunities to do so, but he declined them all. It was not his angle of approach to truth-seeking. It is consistent to believe that Stone's favorite chapter in the Bible was Romans 12: "Live in harmony with one another," and "If possible, so far as it depends on you, live peaceably with all." Stone must have heaped many "coals of fire" on many heads.

But Alexander Campbell was different. He had to be. He wanted to be. He was bold, aggressive. If he was not a "born fighter" he developed the talent. He had to be persuaded to take on his first debate—Walker, 1820. After that he turned back several challengers, but it was not because of any weakness of his, but of theirs. He had the aggressive quality that made men listen to him; whether they agreed or differed, they listened. He was a propagator. But he did this for a Cause; not for himself. He perceived truth clearly, and as a good schoolmaster he made it clear to his hearers. Indeed, as his biographer said, he was a teacher. (So was Stone, for that matter.) He had the advantage over Stone as the leader of a Movement, in that he was aggressive.

1. Campbell's public achievements made him a public figure, almost unrivalled among churchmen of the day. Certainly, Stone had no such eminence as a public figure.

Campbell caught the attention of the church leaders. He challenged "the clergy" in a way they could not ignore. He charged them with pride, arrogance, love of rank, and of recognition of authority. He nettled them. They could not ignore him. Those charges were among the first he made through the *Christian Baptist* in the 1820's, the period generally known as his "iconoclastic period."[1] D. Ray Lindley interpreted this position of his as a reaction against the harsh treatment dealt out to his father by the Synods.[2] In any event he got their attention; the entrenched clergy of his day sat up and listened!

2. He won a genuine, if subdued, respect of the Christian population of America for his victories he won in their behalf. For when Robert Owen, the highly advertised and most widely known agnostic of the day challenged the clergy of America to debate the worth of "religion," including the Christian, the entire clergy of the nation remained silent. Only the obscure editor of a small periodical

---

[1] B.F. Smith's *Alexander Campbell* presents the period as "Literalism" (Chap. II, p. 139ff), others as "Iconoclasm."

[2] *Apostle of Freedom*, the title under which his thesis was published by the Bethany Press in 1957.

in northwest Virginia accepted the challenge.[3] Then he made good on his challenge (in Cincinnati, April 13-23, 1829.) The result was pleasing to all defenders of the Christian religion. "This man Campbell must not be such a heretic after all!"

3. That same year, he indulged in his one venture into the political world. It was not an office that paid, either in funds or influence. He was a successful candidate for the position of a representative of the citizens of his home district, as a delegate to the Constitutional Convention of Virginia. He made a good showing, although he was unable to put over his ideas into the Constitution. The situation was stacked against Western Virginia, by the Tidewater majority of slave-owning aristocracy. But he won the respect of the people for his recognized ability. He was a big enough man to hold his own with the big men of the day. And they were big.[4]

4. His long and prosperous management and ownership of the successful periodicals, The *Christian Baptist* and the *Millennial Harbinger* impressed many, whether they read them or not. He was a successful business man! Also, and not incidentally, he was an outstanding success as a planter. He led in farming methods and in

---

[3] That Challenge which Robert Owen published in New Orleans on January 28, 1826, was not the first contact which Campbell had had with him. R. Fred West in his *Alexander Campbell and Natural Religion* (p. 67) tells of his previous contacts. Campbell had been running a series of articles on "Deism and the Social System," and had been challenged to a debate by a "Doctor Underhill." Campbell declined to meet this "obscure person," but if "his great master, Robert Owen would debate with him he would gladly negate the whole system of his "anti-theistical system." When he read Campbell's reply, he agreed, through the *New Harmony Gazette*, to the debate. In the meantime a copy of Owen's challenge to the clergy of New Orleans had reached Campbell.

[4] Among the "big" men there was ex-President James Madison who, according to Dr. Richardson "spoke in very high terms of the ability shown by him in the convention. 'But,' continued he, 'It is as a theologian that Mr. Campbell must be known. It was my pleasure to hear him very often as a preacher of the gospel, and I regard him as the ablest and most original expounder of the Scriptures I have ever heard.'" (II, 313.)

breeding superior strains of livestock. He must have had some good sense; to be a successful farmer!

5. It might be added that in that generation of fervid, fulsome oratory, Mr. Campbell measured up to the best of the politicians; and that proved to the people that he was a smart man, whatever his theology. On the whole, therefore, Campbell had the general public with him, if it should come to a choice for popularity.

6. Then, the facts of life were with him, as measured against Stone, in recognition as leader of a Cause. Mr. Campbell was younger, lived longer, and retained his powers much later than Mr. Stone. The latter left Kentucky in 1834, moving westward following his children. He was then 62 years of age and quite able. But in 1840 a serious illness threatened his life and a year later a stroke caused paralysis that left his abilities much impaired, at the age of 69, though he lived until he was 72.

Hence, he was out of commission, practically at age 68 when Campbell was still in his early fifties. If Campbell became impaired in vigor at 62 he had ten more years than Stone in his ability to carry on his leadership. For those last critical years, he had the field to himself.

There is no wonder, therefore, why Campbell was recognized as the leader of the Restoration Movement and why the commonplace epithet became "Campbellites."

Moreover, his preponderance persisted after his passing. Dr. Robert Richardson, a fellow faculty member, at Bethany, published *The Memoirs* quite promptly, the second volume within four years after Mr. Campbell's death. The life of Barton W. Stone, on the other hand, waited 88 years after his death, before its publication. In that long gap the story of Stone's spirit and achievements had lost their freshness.[5]

7. During his active, vigorous years, Alexander Campbell did

---

[5] His *Autobiography*, with additions by John Rogers, 1847, had meager circulation; it was incomplete on account of Stone's age and infirmity at the time.

not win praise from the scholars of his day. He was, rather, branded as their enemy. His strictures against the "kingdom of the clergy" assured him of that status. We do not praise our opponents, especially those whom we fear.

Even when he became President and founder of a college, the scholars did not soften toward him. His inhibition against having a "Chair of Theology" in Bethany would prevent that.

Mr. Campbell was really a broad and profound scholar. But his generation of scholars did not recognize that fact. Its recognition awaited a later day. And it came.

The several early generations of preachers in the Reformation, therefore were predominantly of the lower standard of formal schooling. Only a small percent was educated at Bethany. Many local colleges sprang up, however, across the country, established and supported by the brethren of the churches of the Reformation. By the end of the Nineteenth Century there were probably some forty or fifty colleges.

By 1900, some of the graduates of these colleges began to desire what we may call graduate education.

The first "Disciple" student to achieve a degree of Doctor of Philosophy was Clinton Lockhart, who grew up in Illinois and received his undergraduate schooling at the College of the Bible in Lexington, Kentucky and Kentucky University (later Transylvania). From a family of preachers, and talented in scholarship, he went to Yale University, and in 1894 achieved his degree of Doctor of Philosophy.

That same year, 1894, a younger man, Winfred Ernest Garrison got his B.A. degree from Yale. He was the son of Dr. J.H. Garrison, editor of the *Christian-Evangelist*, and one of the most forward-looking [i.e., liberal] ministers of the Brotherhood. He planned to give his son the best education available to anyone. And that son proved to be one of the best and rarest scholars the Cause ever afforded.

W.E. Garrison knew the Brotherhood history and spirit. He and his advisers chose as the theme of his Doctor's dissertation, *The Sources of Alexander Campbell's Theology*.[6] It was the second graduate thesis by a Disciple and it discussed the position of its most eminent leader. (Lockhart's was in the field of Semitics.)

The star of universities moved westward: William Rainey Harper went along and founded the University of Chicago, in 1892. With him went an Aramaic scholar, Herbert Willett, who took his Ph.D. from the University of Chicago. The tide of Disciple studentship followed westward. There were no more Disciple Ph.D.'s from Yale until in the 1940's—then there were several. One was D. Ray Lindley, whose thesis was entitled, *The Structure and Function of the Church in the Thought of Alexander Campbell*, published in 1946. Campbell's star was still shining.

The next was Robert Frederick West, (Ph.D. 1943) with the theme *Alexander Campbell and Natural Religion*, published in 1948. Then came Granville Thomas Walker with *Preaching in the Thought of Alexander Campbell*, in 1948, published in 1954.

Thus, added to the first in 1900, were three in one decade, all on Alexander Campbell. Anyone who gives himself the pleasure and profit of reading these through with rapt attention will testify to the thoroughness and high scholarship ability of each of these Theses. He will also come out with a high respect and deep appreciation for the genuine and broad scholarship of Alexander Campbell. He handled the profoundest of subjects with the hand of a master as he had held his own against some of the greatest antagonists of his day. Those theses, fresh and recent, have refreshed the appreciation of the scholarship of Campbell and built under his reputation even stronger bulwarks for his eminence.

What may prove to be the climax of this modern resurgence of interest in Alexander Campbell in publication of books, has recently appeared in a form both popular and rare; it is Alexander Campbell's career in the form of a novel. It is *The Fool of God*, by Louis

---

[6] This work is available in a new edition from this publisher.—*Editor.*

Cochran, published in 1958. In a brilliant review of this novel,[7] Dr. Perry Epler Gresham obviously has caught the viewpoint and spirit of the present author, for he entitled his review article, "Alexander Campbell Lives Again."

It would be only fair to the picture to list another recent thesis coming out from Yale—one of the other leaders, Barton Warren Stone. This dissertation by William Garrett West[8] has been frequently cited in foregoing chapters. In this recent surge of investigation into the American Reformation of the Nineteenth Century, Stone was not wholly submerged by Campbell. He was recognized. But Campbell still maintained the preeminence.[9]

Here Stone is worthily and accurately presented as an initiator, in the nineteenth century, of the Ecumenical Movement which emerged to the consciousness of the world only in the twentieth.

---

[7] In the *Christian-Evangelist*, April 21, 1958, President Lin D. Cartwright of the Christian Board, and President Perry Gresham of Bethany College both related the fact that Mr. Cochran resided on the campus of Bethany College for many months during the composition of the book, saturating himself in the local traditions of Campbell, (p. 221 f.)

[8] In his book, Dr. West has written some wise comments on the subject of the comparison of the two great leaders, with which the views presented in this chapter are quite harmonious.

[9] Two books on Campbell have been more recently published: Harold Lunger, *The Political Ethics of Alexander Campbell*, and Cecil K. Thomas, *Alexander Campbell and his New Version*. Bethany Press.

CHAPTER XIII
THE PREACHERS OF THE "NEW LIGHTS"

The story of the "New Lights" as told in the previous chapters must have impressed the reader with the turbulency of the time in which this Movement was born. Politically, the Revolutionary War was just over, and the recognition of the new freedom was still just in the process of becoming a part of the thinking of many people. It brought to all a sense of gratitude and release; to many, a feeling of elation and almost intoxication; and to many, confusion. Religiously, the hard fixedness of Calvinism was deeply entrenched in the minds of the theologically inclined and challenged by others who felt the influence of the new release of individual liberty. Socially, the old habitations of the east were being deserted in the surge of migration westward, drawn by the lure of cheap lands and opportunity for a fresh start for the large families. This early period of the Nineteenth Century is known in history as one of extreme views, heated opinions, intense emotions and sharp contentions. In terms of the modern weatherman, it would be described as shifting winds, gusty fronts, tornadoes, funnels, and even cyclones. In the midst of such confusion, moral standards tended to become loosened.

On the other hand, men with convictions were stirred to express them, and by them to influence others. Out of such confusion and turmoil, there arose men of varying types of personality. Some were bold and daring, as pioneers had to be; some were humble and thoughtful as became true Christians; most of them were "rough and ready" as the frontier demanded. Most were unschooled as the circumstances of the frontier compelled them to be.

In the midst of all this turmoil, a small percentage of men were educated, even cultured and devoted, hence they became outstanding leaders, despite their rough exterior. Many of these pioneers, sincerely devoted to their homes and families, desirous of high morals and religion for their wives and growing children, became preachers of the Christian Gospel. Some of them, stirred by the new sense of freedom in America dared to preach, regardless of lack of training and of entrenched standards of historical precedence. Encouraged by the leaders of the new Movement, many a man ventured into the ranks of the preaching brethren, not to say of "the clergy."

To such a type of pioneer manhood, the plea of the "New Light Christians" made a powerful appeal, and many were those who responded to it. Most of these preaching brethren are little known to historical records. Frontiersmen were not given to writing, records were few, and periodicals scarce; sermons were spoken, not written; their effects were in lives, not books. But the number of volunteer preachers was surprising, even the list that has survived in printed records is gratifying, though limited.

These devoted souls deserve to be remembered, even though meagerly. This chapter is devoted to the task of picking up scraps of biography of the preachers of this "New Light" group of pioneers, and pointing to the sources of their available records. About fifty-four of these preachers are mentioned in the available volumes, some quite obscurely; and no doubt many more have not achieved even mentioning. Here we are giving a list of such preachers with meager description and with citation to sources of more extensive records in cases where such are extant and available. It is to be hoped that these sources will be followed up by students and teachers of the Reformation.

Besides these fifty-four, seven fell by the wayside, as related, especially in Chapter V. The most notorious of these, of course, was Richard McNemar, who, at the beginning, appeared to be the foremost in boldness for reform, but who proved to be unstable and probably over-ambitious. His brother-in-law, John Dunlavy, went along with him. Two others who followed were more like "hangers-on": Malcolm Worley and Matthew Houston.

It is believed that the story of these diversions is sufficiently related in Chapter V, with satisfactory citation of sources.

Rice Haggard

Two preachers who proved to be pioneers of great influence came into the Movement along with Barton W. Stone, on the occasion of his official break with the Presbyterians in 1804. These were Rice Haggard, (1769-1819) who had come from the O'Kellyites in Virginia and joined with "Christians" in the 1804 meeting which issued *The Last Will and Testament*. His outstanding contribution was the publication of his tract, *An Address to the Different Religious Societies on the Sacred Import of the Christian Name*, the initiating call for that great concept.

He evangelized extensively in South Kentucky, from his home in Burkesville, and also in Ohio, where he died in 1819. It was a great loss to the Cause that he died when he was only fifty years of age. The story of his life was not published until 1957.[1] His brother, David Haggard of Burkesville, also evangelized throughout south Kentucky, and was clearly a "New Light." All that is known of him is recorded in this same volume.[2]

---

[1] *Rice Haggard: The American Frontier Evangelist Who Revived the Name Christian,* by Colby D. Hall; available in the book *Forgotten Soldier of the Restoration: The Life and Writing of Rice Haggard* (Cobb Publishing, 2020).

[2] There are other references in scattered places to David Haggard. One, by Elder William Kinkade (a biography of whom appears later in this chapter), says: "There have been in the bounds of my acquaintance many miraculous cures performed in answer to prayer. I have been acquainted with several of the people who were healed, conversed on the subject with the persons who were present at the time, and some of these cures I have seen myself. **I as firmly believe that Eld. David Haggard had the gift of healing, as that the apostles had**. He has fallen asleep, but there are many alive who saw him perform cures, and what I saw myself puts the matter beyond doubt with me. I state these facts in honor to God, who, in every age of the world, has shown a willingness to bless his creatures in proportion to their faith and obedience." *Bible Doctrine of God, Jesus Christ, the Holy Spirit, Atonement, Faith, and Election: to which is prefixed some thoughts on natural theology, and the truth of revelation* (New York: H.R. Piercy, 1829) p. 341 (emphasis mine).—Editor.

Clement Nance

Another laborer, from the same source, was Clement Nance (1756-1828) who soon went to the new territory of Indiana, where he became one of the founders of the Movement in that region where the Cause prospered so well in later generations. One of his disciples who became a preacher was James Robeson.

David Purviance

Perhaps the most famous and fruitful of all the Timothies of Stone was David Purviance, who had been a Presbyterian elder at Cane Ridge, prior to Stone's great change, who went with Stone and was ordained by him into the Christian ministry in time for him to become one of the signers of *The Last Will and Testament*. He had obtained an education quite superior for that generation, and served in the state legislature both in Kentucky and Ohio. He led a colony of settlers from Bourbon County (Cane Ridge), Kentucky, into Preble County, Ohio. There he became an outstanding leader, as a reforming preacher and also as a state legislator. The number of young men whom he led into the ministry and ordained is very impressive, as will be told a few pages below.[3]

Samuel Rogers

One of the most fruitful of all the frontier evangelists, both in Kentucky and Missouri, was Samuel Rogers (1789-1872), who had come from a Methodist background and married into a Presbyterian family while living in the Cane Ridge community. There, they all "became attached to [Barton W.] Stone, and by his persuasive eloquence were induced to...go with thousands who, having abandoned the church of their fathers followed the simple teachings of the Holy Scriptures as the only safe and infallible rule of faith and

---

[3] The record of his career was published by his son, Levi Purviance, in 1840, along with a number of other biographies. It is a valuable storehouse of biographies. (NOTE: This work will soon be available in a new edition from this publisher.—*Editor*.)

practice."[4]

Reuben Dooley

Another Stone associate in preaching was Reuben Dooley (1773-1822), a Virginian from a Presbyterian family. He was reared in the wild Kentucky frontier where his schooling was meager, but where the spirit of freedom was such that he rebelled against the Calvinistic teachings of predestination, so turned himself loose, assuming that he was one of the "eternally reprobated" until an evangelistic preacher, Samuel Findlay, stirred his soul to a desire to preach. So eager was this desire that he broke away from the Presbyterian limitations required of their preachers and determined to preach to whom he pleased. This, it turned out, included some Cherokee Indians nearby, where he evangelized fruitfully. At one time he became so destitute of support that he had to trade his hymn book for his ferry fare. He induced David Haggard, "his friend and brother," to take over the preaching of the Indians. He was an intimate friend, too, of Barton W. Stone and traveled with him in evangelizing. His special talent lay in his power of exhortation, which was much used by the "New Lights" of that generation. His early death in 1822 prevented him from knowing of the Campbells, and the fusion. His travels included Illinois and Missouri. It was his fervent exhorting that led to the conversion of Samuel Rogers. His father, Moses Dooley, and his brother Thomas Dooley were gifted in exhortation also, the latter being one of the sweetest singers of the day.

James Crawford

One of the Presbyterian preachers, a Princeton graduate, James Crawford, was won over by Stone and would have been among those present at the Cane Ridge organization meeting in 1804 had

---

[4] As quoted from *Toils and Struggles of the Olden Times: The Autobiography of Elder Samuel Rogers* (p. 31), which is full of pioneer facts and spirit.

it not been for his untimely death in 1803.

Elders of Cane Ridge

Also, in this list should be included those four elders of the Cane Ridge Christian Church who served along with Stone: Moses Hall, Thomas Nesbitt, John Edward, and Samuel Knox. For, in that generation the distinction between elders and preachers was so slight that we may assume that these elders did some evangelizing.

Preacher Students

It is well understood that the school teaching of that early day was done mostly by preachers, because they were well educated and required extra income to support their families. Barton W. Stone, for these reasons was an outstanding teacher. He conducted two private schools that were notable: Lexington, from 1815, and Georgetown after 1819. Some of the young men students, naturally got from him more than book learning; they were inspired to preach the simple Gospel message which he lived and preached. The following six are known to have followed his example in becoming preachers of the new Cause: Leonard J. Flemming, Francis R. Palmer, James Hickman, James Robeson, and also Hamilton Gray, Harrison W. Osborne, and Marcus P. Willis. "Hickman and Gray were early victims of the "White Plague." The remaining seven Christians were leaders of marked ability in Kentucky and contiguous states.[5]

Gano and Allen

Two other students of his in the Georgetown school call for special mentioning: John Allen Gano and Thomas Miller Allen. These two were powerful evangelists. They cooperated in setting up the church in Paris, Kentucky in 1828 and led in the delicate task of the uniting of the Christians and Reformers. Allen, who had

---

[5] C.C. Ware, *Barton W. Stone*, p. 206.

been ordained by Stone in Lexington, went to Missouri in 1836 and was very influential in establishing the Movement in that new state where two other Kentuckians had laid the foundations: Samuel Rogers and Thomas McBride. After seventeen years, he ordained J.W. McGarvey, there.

John Allen Gano used his schooling under Stone in his evangelizing and in his bringing the two groups into union. He was in the company with Stone on his final visit to the old Cane Ridge community. His son, General Richard M. Gano later became a leading pioneer in establishing the Cause in Texas.[6]

John Rogers

A third member of Stone's Georgetown school who became a leading evangelist was John Rogers (1800-1867), a younger brother of Elder Samuel Rogers. John was ordained by Stone in the Georgetown church.

John Rogers had one unique distinction: He was chosen as the representative of the "Christian" group to join with "Raccoon" John Smith from the "Reformers," to "ride among the churches" to encourage them to join their local congregations into one. He evangelized through the several states of Kentucky, Ohio, Indiana, Illinois, Missouri, and Mississippi. His last years were spent as a settled pastor in Carthage, Kentucky. No one was closer to the revered Stone than John Rogers; he was chosen as the Moderator of the famous debate between Alexander Campbell and N.L. Rice in 1843. His record is contained in Levi Purviance's *Biography of David Purviance* and in Barton Stone's *Autobiography*, which he edited.

W.C. Rogers

W.C. Rogers, a nephew of Samuel Rogers, lived and preached

---

[6] This son's short biography of his father, John A. Gano, appears in *The Cane Ridge Meetinghouse* (Cobb Publishing, 2020).

in Missouri, in a later generation, and published a book, *Recollections of Men of Faith*, carrying the traditions of the "New Lights" into the combined group in the new state.

Jesse Bledsoe

In the winter of 1830, the regular congregational meeting of the "Christians" in Lexington was blessed by the confession of faith and baptizing of one of the prominent lawyers of that politically prominent city, Jesse Bledsoe (1776-1836). In 1831 the new building of that congregation was dedicated with this same lawyer giving the dedicatory sermon, for meanwhile he had abandoned his law practice for the Christian ministry. He was reputed to be the most eloquent speaker in Kentucky, granting only one exception, Henry Clay. He became a noted judge and statesman as well as a Gospel preacher.[7]

"Timothies" of David Purviance

Having come over this impressive list of evangelists who had been inspired and/or ordained to preach by Barton W. Stone, let us go back now to one of the earliest of these, David Purviance, and observe the second generation of preachers whom he enlisted in the service. Purviance, having moved to Preble County, Ohio in 1807, enlisted most of these Timothies in that region, but they came from Virginia, Pennsylvania, and Kentucky. Levi Purviance, his own son, is known to us of the later generations best for his publication of the Biography of his father and included in the same volume the biographies of several preachers of the faith. Most of these were "Timothies" of David Purviance, ordained by him and preached out from Preble County, Ohio, where Purviance was the acknowledged leader of the Cause. They preached also from Dayton. These preachers, we will list herewith as a group of "Seven

---

[7] Jesse Bledsoe also served as a US Senator (1813-1814) on the Democratic-Republican ticket, and then as a State Senator for Kentucky (1817-1820).— *Editor.*

preachers who, like David Haggard, died too soon to enter into the fusion."

Thomas Adams

Thomas Adams (1798-1831) son of a Major in the War of 1812 and of the Indian Wars, did his evangelizing out from Dayton, Ohio. As a frontiersman, his education was meager, his manners awkward and his personality somewhat repelling, nevertheless he became a fruitful evangelist by reason of the purity of his heart, and his sincerity in expounding the Gospel. He became a victim of "consumption" and lived only to the age of 33.

William Dyer

Elder William Dyer was ordained to the ministry by Nathan Dooley in 1818. He bade fair to make a useful preacher, but death cut short his life; we have no record of his demise even.

John Hardy

John Hardy (1779-1819) was converted in the year of the great revival, 1801, but he was known as one who "never became enthusiastic," which, doubtless should be interpreted in the light of the excessive zeal of the times; he was known as a "son of consolation." His field of service was in Preble County, Ohio, where the leadership of David Purviance was strong. His service was mostly as a pastor, a type of service which owes its development to this period. He was among those of shortened life, just 40 years.

Thomas B. Kyle

Elder Thomas B. Kyle (1889-c. 1810) was born in Pennsylvania, but lived in Kentucky where his parents were affected by the "great revival"; then moved to Preble County, Ohio, where he preached for a few years under the influence of Purviance, before his premature death in about 1810.

William Kinkaide

William Kinkaide (1783-1832) another short-lived man was raised up as a noted Indian fighter and woodsman, with limited schooling, but after a while in school under Barton W. Stone, proved his superior talents, became quite a linguist, studying Latin and Greek, then Hebrew under a Jewish scholar. His preaching was in Kentucky, Illinois, and Ohio, where he married. He also spent two years in New York, where he published a book called *Bible Doctrine*.[8] The last years of his life in Ohio, he spent as a cripple, and died from tuberculosis. Characteristically he declared "I fellowship with all people of every name without regard to how much they differ from me in doctrine," and "I refused to call myself by any other name than that of Christian." So, he was a true "New Light."

George Shieler

George Shieler (1776-1828) was another "Timothy" of David Purviance, to add to the impressive list, coming from Pennsylvania and moving to Preble County, Ohio, in his early maturity. There he was ordained by Purviance and Abraham Voorhees. He served as an evangelist in Pennsylvania, Ohio, Indiana, and Kentucky, and as a pastor in Preble County.

William Caldwell

Not all of the Ohio contingency of preachers came through the influence of Purviance; Stone himself was responsible for some. On one occasion he made an appointment to preach and to immerse a man by the name of William Caldwell which he did in the Ohio River. While there he brought into the fellowship an entire congregation of Baptists by his plea for Christian union on a New

---

[8] The full title of the work is: "The Bible Doctrine Of God, Jesus Christ, The Holy Spirit, Atonement, Faith, And Election: To Which Is Prefixed Some Thoughts On Natural Theology, And The Truth Of Revelation"—*Editor.*

Testament basis.

Matthew Gardner

Another recruit was Matthew Gardner in Adams County, Ohio, who became so enthused (?) about Stone's plan and his plea that he, later combatted Campbell himself.[9]

John Longley

In the territory of Indiana, likewise, Clement Nance was not the only contribution of Stone to the preaching ministry. John Longley, of Rush County, was conspicuous in the effort to develop the union between the forces of the "Reformed Baptists" and the "Christians," and served as an evangelist.

Elijah Martindale

Elijah Martindale of Henry County, Indiana did much to build this spirit of union. He pleaded for "less emphasis on first principles and more on vital godliness and the indwelling of the Holy Spirit."[10]

Elijah Goodwin

Another pioneer evangelist of the "New Lights" who came into the fusion was Elijah Goodwin (1807-1879). His career is well known by his biography by James Mathes (see Bibliography). His life was spent for the most part in southern Illinois, aside from the stream of travel, but in his late years he became a disciple of Campbell and also active with the Christians.

Jacksonville, Illinois, preachers

---

[9] Matthew Gardner was opposed to the union of forces, and joined instead with the Christian Connexion.—*Editor.*

[10] His life, as well as some humorous anecdotes, can be found in his *Autobiography and Sermons of Elder Elijah Martindale*. It can be read free online at www.TheCobbSix.com/Jimmie-Beller-Memorial-eLibrary/

In 1832 Stone held several evangelistic meetings in Illinois, including one in Jacksonville. In this he was joined by one of his former Georgetown graduates, Harrison W. Osborne and by Josephus Hewitt. In 1834 he moved his home to Jacksonville (largely to escape from a slave state) and moved also his *Christian Messenger*, after a delay. There he was joined in the conduct of this periodical by D. Pat Henderson, whom Stone had immersed back in Fayette County, Kentucky. Henderson continued the paper after Stone's death. "Eleven preachers of the faith receiving this paper at Jacksonville" indicates the strength of the Cause here.

B.F. Hall

Benjamin Franklin Hall (1813-1873), a native of Nicholas County, Kentucky, was a disciple of Barton W. Stone and a fellow-laborer for several decades. The fact that he was also a dentist enabled him to travel widely and preach in many states: Kentucky, Indiana, North Carolina, Tennessee, Alabama, Mississippi, Arkansas, and finally Texas. In the latter state, he participated in the establishment of the Christian Church in at least these centers: Sherman, Van Alstyne, McKinney, Dallas, Fort Worth, and Waco.[11] He was buried in the church yard at Mantua.

The other B.F. Hall

Another B.F. Hall was the founder of the Boulevard Christian Church in Fort Worth: his children are still leaders in the Cause in the vicinity. (There were five Christian preachers by the name of Hall, in the Texas Disciples' ranks, no one kin to another).

Joseph Thomas

Joseph Thomas (1791-1835) was a preaching companion frequently with Barton W. Stone, and an intimate friend. A native of North Carolina, he preached with the brethren throughout Ken-

---

[11] See Hall, Colby D., *Texas Disciples*.

tucky and several states. He was a kind of "lone wolf" in some ways. He was somewhat of a poet—and a dreamer known as "The White Pilgrim," for the long white robe he wore the year round. His first membership was with the "Christian Connection." First sprinkled, then baptized, he was later expelled from them for reasons unknown.[12] He never did join in the fusion with Campbell, although his daughter married a leader of the Indiana organized forces there.

---

[12] Thomas was "baptized" by James O'Kelly in 1807. O'Kelly adamantly insisted that neither pouring nor immersion was baptism, but that sprinkling was. Thus, when in 1811 he was immersed by Elias Smith (of the "Christian Connexion"), and then met with William Guirey (one of O'Kelly's most influential leaders, who later butted heads with him over the sprinkling/immersion issue), it seems quite clear why O'Kelly would "expel" him.—*Editor.*

APPENDIX A
THE LAST WILL AND TESTAMENT OF THE SPRINGFIELD PRESBYTERY

For where a testament is, there must of necessity be the death of the testator; for a testament is of force after men are dead, otherwise it is of no strength at all, while the testator liveth. Thou fool, that which thou sowest is not quickened except it die. Verily, verily I say unto you, except a corn of wheat fall into the ground, and die, it abideth alone; but if it die, it bringeth forth much fruit. Whose voice then shook the earth; but now he hath promised, saying, yet once more I shake not the earth only, but also heaven. And this word, yet once more, signifies the removing of those things that are shaken as of things that are made, that those things which cannot be shaken may remain.—*Scripture.*

THE PRESBYTERY OF SPRINGFIELD, sitting at Caneridge, in the County of Bourbon, being, through a gracious Providence, in more than ordinary bodily health, growing in strength and size daily; and in perfect soundness and composure of mind; but knowing that it is appointed for all delegated bodies once to die: and considering that the life of every such body is very uncertain, do make, and ordain this our last Will and Testament, in manner and form following, viz:

Imprimis. We *will*, that this body die, be dissolved, and sink into union with the Body of Christ at large; for there is but one body, and one Spirit, even as we are called in one hope of our calling.

Item. We *will,* that our name of distinction, with its *Reverend* title, be forgotten, that there be but one Lord over God's heritage, and his name one.

Item. We *will,* that our power of making laws for the government of the church, and executing them by delegated authority, forever cease; that the people may have free course to the Bible, and adopt *the law of the Spirit of life in Christ Jesus.*

Item. We *will*, that candidates for the Gospel ministry henceforth study the Holy Scriptures with fervent prayer, and obtain license from God to preach the simple Gospel, *with the Holy Ghost sent down from heaven*, without any mixture of philosophy, vain deceit, traditions of men, or the rudiments of the world. And let none henceforth take *this honor to himself but he that is called of God, as was Aaron.*

Item. We *will*, that the church of Christ resume her native right of internal government—try her candidates for the ministry, as to their soundness in the faith, acquaintance with experimental religion, gravity and aptness to teach; and admit no other proof of their authority but Christ speaking in them. We will, that the church of Christ look up to the Lord of the harvest to send forth laborers into his harvest; and that she resume her primitive right of trying those *who say they are apostles, and are not.*

Item. We *will,* that each particular church, as a body, actuated by the same spirit, choose her own preacher, and support him by a free-will offering, without a written *call* or *subscription*—admit members—remove offences; and never henceforth *delegate* her right of government to any man or set of men whatever.

Item. We *will,* that the people henceforth take the Bible as the only sure guide to heaven; and as many as are offended with other books, which stand in competition with it, may cast them into the fire if they choose; for it is better to enter into life having one book, than having many to be cast into hell.

Item. We *will,* that preachers and people, cultivate a spirit of mutual forbearance; pray more and dispute less; and while they behold the signs of the times, look up, and confidently expect that redemption draweth nigh.

Item. We *will,* that our weak brethren, who may have been wishing to make the Presbytery of Springfield their king, and wot[1] not what is now become of it, betake themselves to the Rock of

---

[1] Know.—Editor.

Ages, and follow Jesus for the future.

Item. We *will,* that the Synod of Kentucky examine every member, who may be *suspected* of having departed from the Confession of Faith, and suspend every such suspected heretic immediately; in order that the oppressed may go free, and taste the sweets of gospel liberty.

Item. We *will,* that Ja_____, the author of two letters lately published in Lexington, be encouraged in his zeal to destroy *party-ism.* We will, moreover, that our past conduct be examined into by all who may have correct information; but let foreigners beware of speaking evil of things which they know not.

Item. Finally we *will,* that all our *sister bodies* read their Bibles carefully, that they may see their fate there determined, and prepare for death before it is too late.

Springfield Presbytery,
June 25th, 1804.

Robert Marshall,
John Dunlavy,
Richard McNemar,
B.W. Stone,
John Thompson,
David Purviance

APPENDIX B:
CHRONOLOGICAL TIMELINE
OF THE MOVEMENT

The Stone Movement	Year	The Campbell Movement
Barton W. Stone		Alexander Campbell
Stone born 12/24	1772	
Moved to Pittsylvania Co., Virginia	1779	
	1788	Campbell born 9/12
Enters David Caldwell's Academy 2/1	1790	
First Sermon by McGready, Feb. Sermon by Pres. J.B. Smith	1791	
Second Sermon by McGready, "Worried," altered appearance Sermon by Wm. Hodge on "God is love" Stone's "assumed" conversion Candidate for the ministry "Finished course of learning"	1793	
Professor, Succoth Academy, Washington, GA	1795	
Licensed, Orange Presbytery, Spring		
Stone and Foster, missionary tour, N.C., Tempted to go to Florida		
En route: through Knoxville, TN, 8/14 To Kentucky via Lexington Settles: "Close of the year."		
Trial pastor: Cane Ridge & Concord	1796	
Trip to Ga. For Kentucky Academy	1797	
Called: Cane Ridge & Concord, Fall Ordained by Presbytery of Tran-	1798	

150

sylvania, 10/4
At this time taught and believed
   Calvinism, "chilled at con-
   tradiction"		

His "real experience," faith based on testimony	1799	
Renounces Calvinism, "Things move quietly, apathy"	1800	

Inspects McGready's revival in
   Logan County: "bodily exer-
   cises," Spring
Married to Elizabeth Campbell,
   7/2
Preaches his first "New Light"
   sermon at Cane Ridge
Teaches his new views to fel-
   low-evangelists (or sooner)
Great Cane Ridge Revival,
   "Free grace" preached, Aug.
Stone "worked down"
Stone "out-prays" Presbyterian
Stand-pat preacher
Charges against McNemar by
   Washington Presbytery,
   11/11
	1801	

Unwritten charges vs. McNemar in Cincinnati, Oct.	1802	

Synod of Ky: Five withdraw,
   9/7
Revivalist counter-proposals
   rejected, 9/12
	1803	

Springfield Presbytery orga- nized, after September	1803	

Apology printed, and *"Last Will
   and Testament,"* 6/28
Stone ceased infant sprinkling,
   "just before great excite-
   ment"
His two churches stay with him
   as a "New Light" preacher
"Embarrassed by doctrine of
   Atonement"
Stone's "time limited by farm
   work"
	1804	

Shaker's invasion, Spring McNemar and Dunlavy to Shakers	1805	
Stoner's Creek *Immersing* David Purviance moves to Ohio	1807	5/13, Thomas Campbell arrives in Philadelphia from Ireland
Stone's son, Barton Jr., dies	1809	9/29 Alexander Campbell lands in America, New York. 10/25, Joins his father & adopts *Declaration and Address*, which is then published
Marshall & Thompson return to Presbyterians Stone's first wife dies	1810	7/15 Alexander Campbell's first sermon
	1811	3/12, A. Campbell marries Margaret Brown 5/16, A. Campbell's first preaching tour Brush Run church organized
	1812	1/1, A. Campbell ordained 3/3, daughter born 6/12, Campbells immersed
Stone moved to Mansker Creek, TN	1813	Brush Run congregation joins Redstone Baptist Association, Autumn
Stone's *Address to the Christian Churches*	1814	Father-in-Law deeds him a farm
Stone moved to Lexington and resumed pastorate at Cane Ridge Starts a private school in Lexington	1815	
	1816	8/30, Sermon on the Law
Stone bought farm, Georgetown, 11/12	1819	A. Campbell meets Walter Scott
Stone ordained John Rogers, 4/12	1820	Walker Debate
Stone attacked by Thomas Cleland & J.P. Campbell	1814-1822	
	1823	A. Campbell starts the *Christian Baptist* Visits Kentucky for the *McCalla Debate*
Stone & Campbell meet	1824	In Georgetown, Campbell and Stone meet

Stone founds the *Christian Messenger*	1826	
Stone busy evangelizing in Kentucky, Ohio, Tennessee	1827	Walter Scott becomes evangelist for Mahoning Baptist Association Adamson Bentley, Jacob Osborne, Jacob Gaston confer with Scott Scott preaches "baptism for remission" without success
	1827	At New Lisbon, repeats, wins Wm. Amends: "break the ice"
	1829	Campbell-Owen Debate
	1830	12/25-26, Mahoning Association dissolves
Joint meeting of Reformers and Christians: J.T. Johnson and Stone 12/28-31 Joint meeting of Christians and Reformers of Lexington, 12/28-31	1831	Joint meeting of Reformers and Christians: J.T. Johnson and Stone 12/28-31 Joint meeting of Christians and Reformers of Lexington, 12/28-31
Unification of Forces, New Year's Day Stone spends six weeks in Illinois, Fall	1832	Unification of Forces, New Year's Day
John Smith and John Rogers travel among the churches, promoting local unions	1832-1834	John Smith and John Rogers travel among the churches, promoting local unions
	1833	Campbell visits cities in the East
Stone moves to Jacksonville, Illinois, September	1834	
Gave time to preaching tours	1836	Tours Tenn., Ky., then Eastern states
	1837	1/13-17, Campbell-Purcell Debate
	1840	Bethany chartered
Stone suffers a stroke with paralysis	1841	Bethany opened Campbell visits Ky.
Stone writes his *Autobiography*	1843	Campbell-Rice Debate Tours Ohio and Indiana
Stone visits New Paris, Ohio: David Purviance and one night in Cane Ridge	1844	Tours Virginia, South, Missouri, and West

Died at Hannibal, MO, 11/9		
	1847	To England, Scotland, & Ireland
	1849	President, National Convention
	1850	Invited to address Congress Presides as President of Convention
	1851	Lectures in Memphis
	1853	Travels East in behalf of Bethany
	1854	Thomas Campbell dies
	1856	Visits Canada
	1857	Tours through the South
	1858	Tours East in behalf of Bethany
	1859	Tours South for Bethany
	1864	Last trip to General Convention
	1866	Dies at Bethany

BIBLIOGRAPHY

Barrett, Rev. J. Presley. *The Centennial of Religious Journalism.* Dayton: Christian Publishing Association, 1908.

Beardsley, Frank G. *A History of American Revivals.* 3d ed. New York: American Tract Society, 1912.

Boles, H. Leo. *Biographical Studies of Gospel Preachers.* Nashville, Gospel Advocate Co., 1932.

Burnett, David S. *The Christian Baptist.* 7 vols., 1823-1830; condensed into one, 1870.

Campbell, Alexander, editor. *The Christian Baptist*, 1823-1830.

_____ editor. The *Millenial Harbinger*, 1830-1866, continued by Pendleton, Loos and others.

Cobb, Bradley S., editor, *Forgotten Soldier of the Restoration: The Life and Writing of Rice Haggard.* Charleston, AR: Cobb Publishing, 2020.

Garrison, Winfred Ernest. *Religion Follows the Frontier, A History of the Disciples of Christ.* New York: Harper & Bros., 1931.

_____ and DeGroot, Alfred T. *The Disciples of Christ, a History.* St. Louis: Christian Board of Publication, 1948. Revised edition, 1958.

Goodwin, Elijah, *Life of,* by James Mathes, see Mathes.

Hall, Colby D., *Rice Haggard, The American Frontier Evangelist Who Revived the Name Christian.* Fort Worth: University Christian Church, publisher, 1957 Contained in above-mentioned Cobb, editor, *Forgotten Soldier.*

_____ *Texas Disciples.* Fort Worth: Texas Christian University Press, 1953.

Harmon, M.F. *A History of the Christian Church in Mississippi.* Aberdeen, Miss., 1929.

Hayden, A.S. *Early History of the Disciples in the Western Reserve, Ohio.* Cincinnati, Chase & Hall, 1875.

Homan, W.K. *The Church on Trial, or, the McGregor Case.* Dallas: A.D. Aldridge & Co., 1900.

James, William. *The Varieties of Religious Experience.* Modern Library Edition, New York: Random House, 1929.

Kernodle, P.G. *Lives of Christian Ministers, "Over Two Hundred Memoirs."* Author was "Secretary of the Southern Christian Convention." Richmond, Va., 1909.

Lunger, Harold, *The Political Ethics of Alexander Campbell.*

Lindley, D. Ray. *The Apostles of Freedom.* St. Louis: The Bethany Press, 1957.

Luther, Martin. *Works.* Philadelphia: A. J. Holman Co. & The Castle Press, 1932. (In 40 vols.) Vol. VI.

MacLean, J.F. *Life and Labors of Richard McNemar.* Charleston, AR: Cobb Publishing, 2014.

Mathes, James. *The Life of Elijah Goodwin, Pioneer Preacher.* St. Louis: John Burns, 1880.

———— *Works of Elder B.W. Stone.* Cincinnati: Wiltstach, Keys & Co., 1859.

Millennial Harbinger, Alexander Campbell, Editor, 1830-1866. Bethany, W. Va.

Mitchell, N.J. *Reminiscences in the Life of a Pioneer Preacher of the Ancient Order.* Autobiography. Cincinnati: Chase & Hall, 1877.

Purviance, Levi. *Biography of David Purviance, with biographical sketches of Reuben Dooley et al.* Dayton: B.F. & G.W. Ells

[1848] New edition of 1940, with a few additional biographical sketches, (used for all page references).

Richardson, Robert. *Memoirs of Alexander Campbell.* 2 vols. (usually published in one). Philadelphia: J. P. Lippincott, 1868-70.

Rogers, James Edward Haggard, Rice; et al. *The Cane Ridge Meeting House.* Charleston, AR: Cobb Publishing, 2020.

Rogers, John. *The Life and Times of John Rogers of Carlisle, Ky.* One copy only of manuscript, on file in Library of University of North Carolina.

Rogers, Elder Samuel. *Toils and Struggles of the Olden Times: The Autobiography of Elder Samuel Rogers.* Edited by his son, Elder John I. Rogers. Charleston, AR: Cobb Publishing, 2013.

Schaff, Philip. *History of the Christian Church.* 7 vols. New York: Charles Scribner's Sons. Vol. VII. "Modern Christianity. The Swiss Reformation." 3d ed. revised, 1898.

Shaw, Henry. *Buckeye Disciples.* St. Louis: Christian Board of Publication, 1952. A Centennial Publication by the Ohio Christian Missionary Society.

Smith, Benjamin L. *Alexander Campbell.* St. Louis: The Bethany Press, 1930.

Stone, Barton Warren. *The Autobiography of Barton Warren Stone, with additions and reflections by Elder John Rogers.* 5th ed. Cincinnati: J.A. & U.P. James, 1847.

_____*History of the Christian Church in the West.* Reprint from The Christian Messenger of Feb. to Oct., 1827. Lexington, Ky.: The College of the Bible, 1956.

_____*Works of Barton Warren Stone.* Cincinnati: Wiltstach, Keys & Co., 1859.

_____editor, *The Christian Messenger*, 1824-37; 1839-45.

Sweet, William Warren. *Revivalism in America.* New York: Charles Scribner's Sons, 1944.

_____*The Story of Religion in America.* New York: Harper & Bros., 1939 (revised).

Thompson, Rhoades, editor, *Voices from Cane Ridge.* Contains a reprint of the biography of Barton W. Stone. 1954.

Tracy, Joseph. *A History of the Revival of Religion in the Time of Edwards and Whitefield.* Boston: Tappan & Dennet, 1842.

Thomas, Cecil K. *Alexander Campbell and His New Version* 1948 Bethany Press.

Ware, Charles Crossfield. *Barton Warren Stone, a Biography.* St. Louis: The Bethany Press, 1932.

_____*A History of the Disciples of Christ in North Carolina.* St. Louis: Christian Board of Publication, 1927.

Webster's New International Dictionary of the English Language. 2d ed., unabridged. Springfield, Mass.: G. & C. Merriam Co., 1943.

Wells, J.W. *History of Cumberland County (Ky.).* Louisville: The Standard Printing Co., 1947.

West, R. Fred. *Alexander Campbell and Natural Religion.* New Haven: Yale University Press, 1948.

West, William Garrett. *Barton Warren Stone: Early American Advocate of Christian Unity.* Nashville: The Disciples of Christ Historical Society, 1954.

Wilcox, Alanson. *A History of the Disciples of Christ in Ohio.* Cincinnati: Standard Publishing Co., 1918.